Concealed Carry, Stand Your Ground Laws, and the 2nd Amendment Right to Bear Arms

The Beginners Bible for Understanding Constitutional Rights, Gun Ownership & Firearm Self Defense

Austin Tyler

To Mark, Rob, and Aaron

Table of Contents

Introduction

"One of the ordinary modes, by which tyrants accomplish their purposes without resistance, is, by disarming the people, and making it an offense to keep arms." (J. Story, 1840)

Gun ownership is serious business but it's also pretty popular. There are more than 300 million firearms in the United States. That's equivalent to roughly one gun to every man, woman, and child in America. Approximately one-third of American households own at least one gun. That's a whole lot of firearms and it comes with a whole lot of fuss. Gun control, rights, and laws are some of the most hotly debated topics in American society with very strong opinions being slung in every direction about every aspect of guns and gun ownership. Everybody likes to offer their input but what are the real facts of the matter?

Gun laws in the United States can be confusing at the best of times. Many are worded using legal jargon that not even a dictionary will help you to understand. To make matters worse, laws vary by state. The laws and regulations applicable in one state could be completely different from those upheld in neighboring states. Where does this leave you and what are your rights as far as purchasing and using a gun, especially in the case of self-defense?

The aim of writing this book is to help you navigate your way through the basics of the 2nd Amendment right to bear arms, stand your ground laws, and gun ownership as a whole. The aim is to bring some clarity and understanding to the laws surrounding gun ownership and use so that you are better equipped with the knowledge necessary to be a responsible owner and handler. So, what's covered?

- The 2nd Amendment, what the 2nd Amendment is, what led to its creation, and how it affects you and your gun.
- Stand your ground, duty to retreat, castle doctrine, and firearm self-defense
- Concealed carry and its history.
- Gun ownership, gun control, and open carry vs. concealed carry.
- Legal considerations for carrying a firearm.
- Stand your ground, duty to retreat, castle doctrine, and the use of deadly force.
- Self-defense, defense of others, and your rights.
- How to handle a firearm self-defense shooting.
- Responsible gun ownership principles and practices.
- Marksmanship and gun handling.
- Firearm choice and gun operations.
- Firearm maintenance.
- An overview of the differences in open and concealed carry laws by state.
- An overview of the reciprocity between states when traveling with a firearm.

Gun ownership is about more than simply purchasing a firearm for 'just in case" and locking it away in a safe until you need to use it—if you ever need to use it. It is about your rights, the law, and about responsible ownership and use of a deadly weapon. If you are new to gun ownership or are considering buying a gun, you need to have the necessary knowledge to keep yourself, and others, safe. Ignorance of the law and your rights isn't an acceptable defense in the face of trouble that will get you off the hook. Are you ready to take the initiative to be a responsible gun owner, know what your rights and the laws are, and how to properly care for and handle your firearm for your own good and the safety of others? Well, then keep reading and get a handle on the basics of being a good gun owner.

Disclaimer

This book is by no means a training manual for the use of firearms and it is not intended to be used in that way. Simply reading this book does not replace the necessity of expert instruction during certified firearms training. The legal information pertaining to laws, rights, and responsibilities surrounding gun ownership contained within this book is not an exhaustive legal reference and should not be used in lieu of professional legal consultation. The legal information and laws are, to the best of the author's knowledge, correct at the time of writing and publishing but are not guaranteed to be accurate for any length of time thereafter. It is the responsibility of the reader to remain up to date with federal, state, and local laws regarding gun ownership and use. The content of this book is meant to serve as a basic platform upon which to build the reader's knowledge and all legal information should be confirmed by the reader by consulting the laws in their jurisdiction.

Chapter 1:

The 2nd Amendment: A History

Throughout the course of America's rich history, there have been a number of amendments, or changes, made to the Constitution of the United States. What is the Constitution of the United States? It is the supreme law and consists of several articles. It outlines the framework of the national government. The Constitution serves to outline your rights, as a citizen of or visitor to the country, and the rights of the government.

It was first enforced in 1789 and while many states had ratified the Constitution, or agreed to it, without amendments, not everything is perfect the first time it is rolled out. There have been a total of 27 amendments made to the constitution to date since its inception. As times change, so does the Constitution. This is evident in one of the amendments being made to revoke a previous amendment so that the Constitution could continue meeting the needs of an evolving nation beyond the 18th century. The first 10 amendments, together, are known as the Bill of Rights. These offer particular protection of justice and individual liberty by placing restrictions on the government's power over the nation. Later, further amendments were made to expand on the protection of individual civil rights while others were made to combat and correct problems in relation to federal authority or amend processes and procedures in government.

Did you know: The original United States Constitution was four pages long and written on parchment paper. Unlike amendments made to any other constitution in the world, amendments to the United States Constitution are added to the original document.

The first three words of the United States Constitution are 'We, the People" which serves to reinforce that the United States government exists to serve the people of the country. The constitution has been enforced for over two centuries, balancing the power of government and safeguarding the interests of majority rule and the rights of minorities, protecting equality and liberty for all, and protecting the interests of state and federal governments. The United States Constitution has even influenced the constitutions of other countries across the globe.

What Is the 2nd Amendment?

Now that we've explained what the constitution is and why it's enforced, let's look at the 2nd Amendment and how it came into being.

The 2nd Amendment serves to preserve your right to keep and bear arms. What does that mean, exactly? The right to keep and bear arms in the United States is considered a fundamental right. Fundamental rights are defined as a group of rights within a constitution that is highly protected from being encroached or infringed upon. At face value, the right to keep and bear arms simply means that you have the right to own and use weapons but we all know that things are rarely as simple as they appear at first glance.

The 2nd Amendment states:

"A well-regulated militia, being necessary to the security of a free State, the right of the people to keep and bear arms, shall not be infringed." (Wikipedia, 2020)

The term militia refers to non-professional armed forces that may be called upon in a time of need. This armed force differs from traditional, full-time military personnel in that they are not necessarily professionally trained or qualified in weapons handling to a military level. Members of the militia are also not permanently kept as an armed force whereby that is their only job. A militia is not able to stand its ground against the likes of regular professional armed forces and in times of need only support those professional forces if and where needed. Local laws also often limit the service of a militia to only their local region and only for a limited period of time. A militia can also be defined in a simpler way as the total able-bodied population of an area, be it a community, a town, a state, or the entire country, which can be called to arms in a time of need.

In the modern world, militias are uncommon in the developed world to a large degree, and the need to keep and bear arms to support a "well-regulated militia" has all but fallen away completely. The 2nd Amendment has not fallen away with that need and is also often taken out of context. To understand the true context, we must dig up some of the historical dirt on this amendment to the Constitution.

Pre-Constitutional Influences

America and the laws governing the states and country didn't just emerge out of nowhere. Many of the laws that have been passed in American history have been influenced by those of other countries. One such country is England as the original 13 states of America were built upon what were the 13 British colonies prior to the American Revolution. The United States Bill of Rights is based partly on and influenced by the English Bill of Rights which precedes the United States Constitution by approximately 100 years.

The 1689 English Bill of Rights

In English history, the Protestants' right to bear arms is considered, in English law, to be a subordinate auxiliary right. This auxiliary right supported the right to personal liberty and resistance to oppression, the right to personal security, and the right to private property and the protection thereof.

In 1689, the English Bill of Rights came into being as a result of a turbulent political period. During this period two significant issues became a major source of conflict. The first was the authority of the King to govern and disarm his subjects without obtaining consent from Parliament. The second was the ever-growing tension between the Protestant citizens and the role of monarchy in England. During the Glorious Revolution, King James II was overthrown and his successors accepted the terms set out in the English Bill of Rights. One of the issues that the Bill resolved was the traditional authority of the King to disarm his subjects. This was a landmark change in the law as prior to the Bill, King Charles II and King James II had enjoyed free reign to unscrupulously disarm Protestant subjects that were deemed known to or suspected of disliking or disagreeing with the government. Furthermore, the King had also presented an argument to Parliament in favor of maintaining a permanent army.

In the Bill, the declaration is made that it is restoring "ancient rights" that were squashed by King James II. It was intended that the right to keep and bear arms as part of a militia will be preserved and that Protestant militias in England at the time would not be disarmed. Inadvertently, the historic plight of Protestants in England helped to shape the United States Constitution as we know it today.

Pre-Constitutional Experiences In America

Early on, when the English began to settle in America, they considered the right to keep arms and/or the right to bear arms and/or the implementation of state militias to be important for one or more of several reasons:

- Support the fundamental right of self-defense.
- Law enforcement participation.
- Enabling the organization of a militia system.
- Warding or fighting off an invasion.
- Preventing oppression from a tyrannical government.

- Suppressing the chances of rebellion—this is a hotly debated reason for valuing the right to keep and bear arms as some speculate that it includes the ability to suppress slave rebellions.

It is uncertain and widely disputed which of these reasons for keeping and bearing arms was considered to be of great importance. Therefore, it is not clear which were meant to be expressed in the creation of the 2nd Amendment. However, some clues as to which reasons were valued above others can be found in mentions for early state constitutions. An example is the 1776 Pennsylvania State Constitution which states "the people have a right to bear arms for the defense of themselves and the state." (Wikipedia, 2020)

During the pre-revolutionary period in the 1760s, colonists made up the established colonial militia. Many of these colonists were still loyal to the British imperial rule. However, things weren't all sunshine and roses and the British rule in American colonies faced an increase in defiance and opposition. Colonists throughout the colonies became divided into two camps, the Loyalists who supported the British rule and the Patriots who desired independence from that rule. Throughout the colonial militias, distrust grew between these two opposing sides which resulted in some Patriots branching off to create their own militias, effectively excluding the Loyalists from those militias. Subsequently, the Patriot militias sought to stock up armories of their own.

The British Parliament responded to this potential threat of rebellion within the colonies by blocking the supply of firearms, ammunition, and parts to the American colonies. Furthermore, King George III set out disarming individuals located in the most rebellious colonial areas during the 1760s and 1770s. If you think that this seems like a complete contradiction to the English Bill of Rights, you are right.

The Loyalist action taken in the early days of the American Revolution was to disarm independent Patriot militia armories. This didn't sit well with the Patriots who cited the Declaration of Rights, William Blackstone's Declaration of Rights summary, the laws of their own militias, and the English common law right to self-defense. As you can see, prior to and during the American Revolution the need for the 2nd Amendment was already there but what was to be done about it now?

After all was said and done and the American Revolution was fought and won, the United States of America gained independence from British Rule. The original 13 states of America were governed by what was known as the Articles of Confederation or the first Constitution. This presented a problem for America because each of the 13 states was responsible for its own governance except for a weak central federal government or Congress which was only granted a small amount of power which the original British colonies recognized as belonging to Parliament and the King. As a result, the standing or permanent army dwindled down to next to nothing which rendered the federal military presence ineffective. Having such a weak military caused instances of state-localized rebellion, such as the western Massachusetts armed tax rebellion, which was unmanageable from a federal level.

Once again, the American people were divided into two camps. There were the Federalists who supported a strong central government power. Then there were the Anti-Federalists who opposed a strong central governing power in favor of states having more independent governing power over their own territories.

The Federalists highlighted an ineffective division of power between the states and Congress and the resulting military weakness. On the other hand, the Anti-Federalists sympathized with the rebels and favored limiting the power of Congress. As a result, the Constitutional Convention was held in 1787 and it proposed that Congress be awarded exclusive authority to create and maintain a permanent army and navy presence with no restrictions on the size thereof. This didn't sit well with the Anti-Federalists who balked against shifting power from the separate states to the federal government. However, as it became increasingly clear that the Constitution would be adopted across the board, they changed tactics. Instead of rebelling against increasing federal government power, they pressed for establishing the

Bill of Rights which would help to limit the power of the federal government and avoid militias from being disarmed.

So, what does all of this mean? The Constitution of the United States grants a central government a great deal of power to govern the nation. The Bill of Rights prevents this power from being absolute by granting rights to the people, allowing them the right to keep and bear arms so that a "well-regulated militia" may be maintained. Thus, the people have the right to protect their liberties and resist oppression from an unjust government. It's all about balancing power between the people, state governance, and a central government.

Notable Debates on Constitution Amendment

As you can imagine, the amendment of the constitution was a hotly debated topic with parties that were both for and against the amendments. The reason these debates are important to consider when understanding these amendments is due to the language used and what it, therefore, meant to the people who wrote and approved of the Constitution and the amendments. Here are some of the most notable debates surrounding the proposed amendments.

State Power Argument

Opposition to the new Constitution was considerable as it transferred power from state militias to the federal government. The concern here was that neglecting the militia may allow the federal government to amass a formidable military that could overpower the militia. What this may cause is an encroachment on the powers of the states, conflicts, and confrontation with the states, and even a possible takeover by the military. Article VI of the old Constitution or the Articles of Confederation reads:

"No vessel of war shall be kept up in a time of peace by any State, except such number only, as shall be deemed necessary by the United States in Congress assembled, for the defense of such state, or its trade; nor shall any body of forces be kept up by any state in time of peace, except such number only, as in the judgment of the United States, in congress assembled, shall be deemed requisite to garrison the forts necessary for the defense of such state; but every state shall always keep up a well-regulated and disciplined militia, sufficiently armed and accoutered, and shall provide and constantly have ready for use, in public stores, a due number of field pieces and tents, and a proper quantity of arms, ammunition, and camp equipage." (Wikipedia, 2020)

This means that no state may have a permanent military or naval presence during times of peace that was more than necessary for the protection of that individual state's protection and protection of trade.

In contrast to the Articles of Confederation, the new Constitution, Article I, Section 8, Clause 16 reads:

"To provide for organizing, arming, and disciplining the militia, and for governing such Part of them as may be employed in the service of the United States, reserving to the States respectively, the appointment of the officers, and the authority of training the militia according to the discipline prescribed by Congress." (Wikipedia, 2020)

What this translates to is that the state training of the militia must be in accordance with federal government guidelines, which may be biased to afford superior military training, and that part of the power of the federal government is the power to govern certain parts of state militias. Take that into consideration with the power of the federal government to amass a permanent military and navy of unlimited size. You then have a recipe that gives the federal government the ability to overwhelm state militias, one of the purposes of which is to resist oppression. This did not sit well with those who were not confident in the federal government's ability to be fair, just, and uphold the liberties of the people.

Tyrannical Government

One of the principal concerns about creating an incredibly powerful central government was the risk of corruption within the federal government and the resulting possibility of unjust oppression and autocracy. Federalists were accused, by the opposition, of fashioning a dictatorial government, and even they had to carefully acknowledge the risk.

Those writing the Constitution viewed the 2nd Amendment as a potential safeguard against oppression. Theodore Sedgwick stated this shared thought when stating the formation of the federal government is "a chimerical idea to suppose that a country like this could ever be enslaved ... Is it possible ... that an army could be raised for the purpose of enslaving themselves or their brethren? Or, if raised whether they could subdue a nation of freemen, who knows how to prize liberty and who have arms in their hands?" (Wikipedia, 2020)

After the approval of the Constitution, but before the first Congress was elected, James Monroe included in his writings "the right to keep and bear arms" as part of a list of fundamental "human rights" and proposed that it be added to the Constitution.

Slave Patrol Preservation

Slave patrols consisted of groups of armed white men who were tasked with monitoring and maintaining discipline enforced upon black slaves. Thom Hartmann, a political commentator, stated that Patrick Henry, James Madison, and George Mason had concerns over slave patrols being threatened if disarmed. Due to this concern, the Constitution would need to clarify the right of states to organize slave patrols which were equated with militias. In addition to this opposition, Patrick Henry expressed opposition against approval of both the Constitution and the 2nd Amendment as it was a requirement for the majority of white men of the southern states between the ages of 18 and 45 to serve in slave patrols.

Note: Paul Finkelman, a legal historian, argues against the claim Hartmann made that the adoption of the 2nd Amendment was a result of the necessity to protect slave patrols as misleading and factually incorrect. His argument further states that no historical evidence exists to support this claim.

Drafting and Adopting the 2nd Amendment

The Articles of Confederation were clearly inefficient and had to be remedied. The Mount Vernon Conference was held in March of 1785 at which delegates from Maryland and Virginia were in attendance to seek a solution. In 1786, 12 delegates from five of the 13 states came together in Annapolis, Maryland for the same purpose. These five states were New York, New Jersey, Virginia, Delaware, and Pennsylvania. At this meeting, a list of issues with the current government structure was drawn up and another meeting in Philadelphia was arranged to be held in May 1787. At this meeting solutions to the current government, structure issues would be presented.

The issues that needed solving included:

- A lack of an interstate arbitration process that would deal with disagreements between separate states.
- A lack of adequately armed and trained interstate security personnel to keep rebellions in check.
- The lack of a national militia to ward off invasions from foreign countries.

The most apparent solution to the problem was to hand control of the militias within the separate states over to the federal Congress and grant Congress the authority to develop a permanent army. This is exactly what the Federalists had wanted from the start. These changes were set out in Article 1, Section 8 of the Constitution. The changes would allow Congress to:

- Develop and support armies, even though no money would be set aside for that purpose would be for more than two years.
- Develop and maintain a navy.
- Organize militia to uphold the law, keep rebellions in check, and ward off foreign invasion.
- Organize, arm, and discipline a militia.
- Govern parts of militia that may be employed to serve the United States. However, the appointment of officers and training of the militia according to the guidelines set out by Congress to the respective states.

There were some delegates present who mistrusted the proposed power shift. They were concerned about the natural risks involved in creating a centralized power. On the one hand, the Federalists, one of which was James Madison, started off by arguing that the Bill of Rights wasn't necessary. They were confident that the federal government would never be able to develop a permanent army powerful enough to overwhelm a militia. Noah Webster, also a Federalist, presented the argument that an armed population wouldn't find it difficult to stand up to a possible threat to their liberty that a permanent army may pose.

The opposing Anti-Federalists pushed back against the Federalists. They insisted on amending the Constitution to include more clearly defined and itemized rights that placed clearer restrictions on this new central government power. They feared that the federal government would decide to take control of the state militias, removing the power of the people to resist oppression and loss of their liberties.

Again the Federalists stepped forward with the counterargument that listing only specific rights would lead to those rights that were not listed to go unprotected. However, they soon came to realize that there wasn't enough support to validate and agree on the Constitution without the Bill of Rights. Federalists had to give in and agree to support the amendment of the Constitution to include the Bill of

Rights after the Constitution was adopted. This promise was enough to convince enough of the Anti-Federalist delegates to vote in favor of the Constitution and it was announced as agreed upon and approved on the 21st of June, 1788. Nine of the 13 states had initially agreed to the adoption of the Constitution and the remaining four would later do the same but Rhode Island and North Carolina would only do so after the Constitution had been amended and the Bill of Rights had been passed and sent to them for approval.

The same Federalist who argued against the Bill of Rights, James Madison, drafted the Bill of Rights. It was proposed by Congress on the 8th of June 1789 and adopted on the 15th of December 1791.

Producing the Bill of Rights

Producing the final Bill of Rights was no walk in the park. There was a lot of to and fro and various amendments were made to the 2nd amendment before it came to be what it is today.

When James Madison initially proposed the Bill of Rights to the House of Representatives on the 8th of June 1789, the 2nd Amendment read:

"The right of the people to keep and bear arms shall not be infringed; a well-armed and well-regulated militia being the best security of a free country: but no person religiously scrupulous of bearing arms shall be compelled to render military service in person." (Wikipedia, 2020)

On the 21st of July, Madison brought up the issue of the Bill yet again and this time put the proposal forward that a committee should be created to report on the development of the Bill. The House of Representatives voted favorably and the Bill of Rights went to a committee to be reviewed. A reworded version of the 2nd Amendment was returned to the House of Representatives on the 28th of July and now it read:

"A well-regulated militia, composed of the body of the people, being the best security of a free State, the right of the people to keep and bear arms shall not be infringed; but no person religiously scrupulous shall be compelled to bear arms." (Wikipedia, 2020)

In August, the House of Representatives further debated and again modified the 2nd Amendment. The debates were centered around the possible risk or government mal-administration by making use of the 'religiously scrupulous" clause to do away with militia just as Great Britain had tried to do away with the militia at the start of the American Revolution. The final clause was modified to address this concern and on the 24th of August the House of Representatives provided the Senate with a version of the 2nd Amendment that reads:

"A well-regulated militia, composed of the body of the people, being the best security of a free state, the right of the people to keep and bear arms shall not be infringed; but no one religiously scrupulous of bearing arms shall be compelled to render military service in person." (Wikipedia, 2020)

On the 25th of August, when the Senate received the amendment, it was entered into the Senate Journal. However, there was one small problem. The Senate scribe didn't take down the passage exactly as the House of Representatives had worded it. Instead, a comma was added before "shall not be infringed" and the semicolon separating that particular phrase from the religious exemption clause was replaced by a comma. This could potentially change the entire context of the amendment.

At this point in time, the proposal of the right to keep and bear arms was an amendment unto its own as opposed to being incorporated into a single collective amendment with other rights, such as the right to due process. A representative explained that this would allow each amendment to be agreed upon and adopted as a distinct amendment to the constitution by each of the states.

On the 4th of September, the Senate changed the language of the 2nd Amendment. This time they removed the definition of militia "composed of the body of the people" and the "religiously scrupulous" clause.

On the 9th of September, the Senate changed the 2nd Amendment wording yet again. The proposal to add "for the common defense" before "bear arms" was turned down. Additionally "the best" was replaced with "necessary to the". The Bill of Rights was sent back to the House of Representatives and it read:

"A well-regulated militia being necessary to the security of a free state, the right of the people to keep and bear arms, shall not be infringed." (Wikipedia, 2020)

On the 21st of September, 1789, the House of Representatives accepted the reworded version of the 2nd amendment as changed by the Senate.

Eventually, the final rendition of the Bill of Rights, consisting of the first 10 amendments made to the Constitution, was adopted. By this time the original 13 states had grown to 14 states and the Bill of Rights was agreed upon and approved by 75% of those states, the exceptions being Massachusetts, Connecticut, and Georgia. These remaining states eventually agreed and approved the amendments in 1939.

The 2nd Amendment Today

Considering that the 2nd Amendment was ratified over 200 years ago, how does that impact the interpretation of it in modern America today?

The 2nd Amendment was heavily influenced by the English Bill of Rights as it pertained to the Protestants at the time. That text is often taken out of context and only quoted as a single line out of the passage: "That the subjects which are Protestants may have arms for their defense suitable to their conditions and as allowed by Law." (Wikipedia, 2020) This may lead to the Bill being misconstrued as providing the right to keep and bear arms for self-defense. Instead, when read fully, the intent is clearly to prevent the unlawful disarmament of Protestants by the crown. The original intent of the English Bill of Rights was incorporated into the 2nd Amendment so that it reflects the same meaning. Effectively, the 2nd Amendment does not give you the right to have arms in self-defense; it only serves to protect your right against disarmament when defending your liberties against oppression. This link, historically, between the English Bill of Rights and the 2nd Amendment, both of which set out the protection of an existing right to protect your liberties instead of creating a new one, is acknowledged by the United States Supreme Court.

It is accepted that the right to self-defense is a Constitutional common-law right and, therefore, was not taken into consideration when the English Bill of Rights was drawn up. Therefore, it was also not taken into consideration as part of the intent behind the 2nd Amendment and as such the 2nd Amendment did not originally grant a person the right to keep and bear arms for self-defense. It applied only to having and carrying weapons while participating in an organized militia. However, that was all about to change after the turn of the 21st century.

It wasn't until the case of District of Columbia v. Heller in 2008 that the Supreme Court of the United States announced that the right to keep and bear arms applied to individual persons in relation to self-defense within their homes. This was seen as a landmark declaration as it affirmed for the very first time that the 2nd Amendment guarantees an individual the right to keep and bear arms for self-defense within an individual's home and not just to protect their liberties as part of a militia. It also included in that declaration that the right is not unlimited; the right does not negate well-established prohibitions, such as the "the possession of firearms by felons or the mentally ill" being illegal. Nor does the declaration negate the prohibition of "the carrying of dangerous and unusual weapons." In the case of McDonald v. City of Chicago in 2010, the Supreme Court ruled that local and state governments are bound from infringing on this right to the same degree as the federal government. To do so, the Due Process Clause of the 14th Amendment was clarified. The 14th Amendment's Due Process Clause is the state's legal obligation to respect an individual's legal rights, including the 2nd Amendment. The legal right in question, as it relates to the newly established interpretation of the 2nd Amendment, being the right to self-defense. Furthermore, in 2016 and the case of Caetano v. Massachusetts, the Supreme Court ruled that the 2nd Amendment extended to all weapons that can be considered to be bearable arms. It is not restricted to only those weapons available at the time of the founding, nor is it restricted to only those weapons that may be useful in warfare.

In a nutshell, despite the 2nd Amendment being put into effect more than two centuries ago, it has only recently been recognized as pertaining to individuals for self-defense within their homes. It has also only recently been declared that all three tiers of government, local, state, and federal are prohibited from infringing upon that right to the same extent. However, this does not mean that all laws regulating the right to keep and bear arms are exactly the same across all states. Finally, the right to bear arms isn't restricted only to the weapons available when the amendment was made, nor does it solely apply to weapons that are only useful for military use.

Chapter 2:

Concealed Carry: A History

Concealed carry is also referred to as carrying a concealed weapon (CCW). The term is quite self-explanatory. Concealed carry refers to carrying a weapon, a handgun, or other, in public in such a way that it is hidden from view. Concealed carry can be a weapon carried on your person or close by. Concealment of a weapon doesn't just extend to an ankle holster or a shoulder holster under a jacket. It also refers to any method of carrying a firearm that is not visible to the eye. Such methods may include carrying a firearm in a bag or even in the trunk of a car. Carrying a concealed weapon is regulated by different laws in different countries and jurisdictions. It is imperative to always check the local and state laws wherever you are to ensure that you are compliant. In various states, legally carrying a concealed weapon requires the person to acquire a permit. However, this is not always the case with law enforcement. Law enforcement usually carries weapons visibly but in the case of plainclothes or undercover agents, they may need to conceal their weapon. Concealed carry is the direct opposite of open carry, where you carry a weapon in such a way that it is plainly visible to those around you.

Early Concealed Carry Bans

When America was first colonized, there were no laws surrounding carrying a concealed weapon. The original 13 states took their cue from the English common law of the 13 English colonies they replaced.

Generally speaking, English common law prohibits the carrying of a concealed weapon.

The first laws to be passed regarding concealed carry were bans. Kentucky and Louisiana were the first states to ban concealed carry, passing the bans in 1813. More states followed suit during the course of the 19th century. Various concealed carry bans were passed before the introduction of the revolver in 1835. Before the revolver came onto the scene, guns were much more difficult, if not impossible, to carry concealed on your person. Therefore, many of these early pre-revolver bans were mostly aimed at prohibiting the concealed carry of other weapons such as knives. Obviously, there were many bans passed after the advent of the revolver but the origin of concealed carry bans stems from non-firearm weapon concerns.

By the end of the antebellum period, almost all of the Southern states had implemented concealed carry bans. This is an interesting occurrence. The antebellum period spanned between the end of the War of 1812 to the start of the Civil War in 1860. During this period there was an immense amount of transformation within the states. Before this, the northern and southern states have economies that were built upon variety. The Industrial Revolution led the northern states to specialize their economy around manufacturing. At the same time, a cotton boom in the south made that the main pillar of the Southern states' economies. During this cotton boom, slavery was rife and it is controversially speculated that concealed carry bans in some states were influenced by slavery. The speculation is that banning the carry of concealed weapons would effectively disarm slaves and prevent slave rebellion. It must be noted that this is only speculation and is not factually proven.

Concealed Carry and the 2nd Amendment

The first time a Supreme Court case addressed the issue of concealed carry bans in relation to the 2nd Amendment was in the case of Robertson v. Baldwin in 1897. The defendant, Robert Robertson, claimed that being detained by a California marshal and the plaintiff in the case, Barry Baldwin, for possessing a concealed firearm violated his 2nd Amendment right to keep and bear arms. While the case was being deliberated, Robertson presented the argument that the 2nd Amendment granted him the right to carry a concealed firearm. However, the court ruled otherwise. The court found that the 2nd Amendment allowed the defendant the right to carry a firearm but not to conceal it.

Why is this case notable in the history of gun control in America? It played an important role in the development of the statutes and regulations surrounding the 2nd Amendment. The first thing it did was bring to light that there was a part of the 2nd Amendment that needed addressing; namely, the carrying of concealed firearms. This court case opened up the door to new thoughts about the idea of carrying a concealed weapon. It also allowed differentiation between the various laws pertaining to the 2nd Amendment and brought about a new legislature in America.

Due to the Robertson v. Baldwin case, today's laws regarding possession and open and concealed carry are distinctly clear, unlike the confusion surrounding them at the time. Ultimately, this case is a landmark case that put in motion the development of open carry permits, concealed carry permits, and various other laws that specify what an individual's right is when carrying a firearm.

Firearms and Vermont

In almost every state you travel to in America, there will be some form of general gun law or another, whether it be permits or bans on concealed carry, licensing laws, or others. However, there is one state that is a notable exception to the rule is Vermont.

Formerly, the state of Vermont had next to no gun control laws in place. This changed somewhat in 2018 when the state changed the laws. Private gun sales required a background check. The minimum age for purchasing a firearm was raised to 21. The exception to this rule is purchasing a long gun from a non-federally licensed firearm dealer. In this case, the age is set at 16 and the purchaser must present the seller with a satisfactory completion certificate for a hunting safety course and the course must be approved by Vermont's Commissioner of Fish and Wildlife. Vermont also banned the possession or sale of handgun magazines that held more than 15 bullets and rifle magazines that held more than 10 bullets. The possession of bump stocks was banned and the police were granted permission to try to obtain a court order which would allow them to seize firearms from anyone who was deemed a serious risk. An individual is allowed to both open and concealed carry without the necessity of a permit. This is also known as constitutional carry in the United States since your 'permit' to carry is the constitution itself.

What helped shape this relaxed approach to gun laws? It is noted that Vermont is a relatively rural state that boasts strong outdoor sport and hunting traditions. It's rural character and firearm-centric traditions have helped to cultivate the state's historically renowned passive firearm laws.

Did you know: Vermont gun law does not differentiate between state residents and visitors. Both residents and visitors are permitted to carry a firearm permit-free while they are within Vermont state lines.

Concealed Carry Bans and Racial Discrimination

As previously stated, there were various states, notably the Southern states, which passed concealed carry bans. However, these laws were not to be enforced against white individuals. Instead, they were only to be enforced against African-Americans in a bid to disarm the African-American population. The states went about this in a clever way because the ban did not explicitly state that it was only to be enforced against African-Americans and not against the white population. Why not state it plainly? The simple answer is the 14th Amendment which reads:

"All persons born or naturalized in the United States, and subject to the jurisdiction thereof, are citizens of the United States and of the state wherein they reside. No state shall make or enforce any law which shall abridge the privileges or immunities of citizens of the United States; nor shall any state deprive any person of life, liberty, or property, without due process of law; nor deny to any person within its jurisdiction the equal protection of the laws." (Wikipedia, 2020)

What this means is that by not explicitly stating that African-Americans were to be singled out for the enforcement of this law, they went about it quietly behind the scenes. This equates to purposeful and unlawful discrimination.

Associate Justice of the Florida Supreme Court, Rivers H. Buford said of Florida concealed carry ban: "the original Act of 1893 ... was passed for the purpose of disarming the negro laborers ... and to give the white citizens in sparsely settled areas a better feeling of security. The statute was never intended to be applied to the white population and in practice has never been so applied. ... It is a safe guess to assume that more than 80% of the white men living in the rural sections of Florida have violated this statute. It is also a safe guess to say that not more than 5% of the men in Florida who own pistols and repeating rifles have ever applied to the Board of County Commissioners for a permit to have the same in their possession and there has never been, within my knowledge, any effort to enforce the provisions of this statute as to white people, because it has been generally conceded to be in contravention to the Constitution and non-enforceable if contested." (Wikipedia, 2020)

If you think that Florida was the only state to actually 'state the obvious', then you are sorely mistaken, and it wasn't the most explicit either.

The previous Florida Constitution of 1838, as well as the Tennessee Constitution of 1834 and the Arkansas Constitution of 1836, stated: "That the free white men of this State shall have a right to keep and to bear arms for their common defense." (Wikipedia, 2020) These early concealed carry laws were extremely and explicitly racially discriminatory by way of loopholes within the laws as they were written but it wasn't to last. Eventually, the fight for racial equality would see definitions of who may or may not be persecuted under concealed carry bans changed.

Paving the Way for Concealed Carry Licensing

When the 20th century began, there were lots of restrictive laws governing handguns. A particularly notable law was the 1911 Sullivan Law of New York which necessitated a permit for just owning a handgun. What does this have to do with concealed and open carry laws? Well, it paved the way for changes in licensing across the country.

Sullivan laws and statutes passed by other states created a licensing process for concealed carry as opposed to banning it altogether. Within these laws, carrying a concealed firearm without a license became a misdemeanor. Not only that, restrictive may-use licensing was brought in which is still found in some jurisdictions today. Law enforcement was not covered by these licensing laws, however, those who were of "good character" and who showed good cause for needing a concealed carry license could obtain a permit. Often, these permits weren't issued unless the applicant was wealthy and well-connected in political circles. Furthermore, they were rarely granted to individuals who weren't white males. Again, the granting of permission for such licenses was discriminatory but, in this case, the discrimintion was both racial and classist. Not the law itself as written, that is sound. However, there are various working parts to such a system and each part may have its own opinion, perception, and even prejudice to bring to the table. Unfortunately for the non-wealthy and non-white population, being able to contest an unfair rejection of application for a license wasn't possible due to a lack of socio-political clout and funds to fuel a court case.

There is good news among all of this political turmoil surrounding licensing laws and actually granting the permits. There were more liberal states who were more relaxed in their licensure.

In 1923, New Hampshire passed the first-ever "shall-issue" law under which an applicant must be issued a permit if legal requirements are met.

In 1961, Washington went down the same path.

Finally, in 1969, Connecticut came to the party as well and still technically remains a "may-issue" state.

Concealed Carry Licensing Wave One

- 1987: Florida converted from "may issue" to "shall issue."
- 1989: Georgia, Oregon, Pennsylvania, West Virginia converted from "may issue" to "shall issue" and Tennessee converted from "no issue" to "may issue."
- 1990: Idaho converted from "may issue" to "shall issue" and Mississippi went from "no issue" to "shall issue."
- 1991: Montana converted from "may issue" to "shall issue."
- 1994: Colorado and Tennessee ("may issue" since 1989) converted from "may issue" to "shall issue". Alaska and Arizona went from "no issue" to "shall issue."
- 1995: Nevada, Utah, Virginia converted from "may issue" to "shall issue". Texas, Arkansas, Oklahoma, North Carolina converted from "no issue" to "shall issue."
- 1996: Louisiana and South Carolina convert from "may issue" to "shall issue". Kentucky converted from "no issue" to "shall issue."

At the end of the first wave of concealed carry law reform, the entirety of the Deep South had converted to "shall issue" and the number of states adopting a "shall issue" approach totaled 30. There were only seven states left who still upheld a "no issue" approach to concealed carry licensing.

- 2001: Michigan converted from "may issue" to "shall issue."
- 2003: Alaska revoked its restriction of concealed carry, making it the second state to declare unrestricted concealed carry. However, this differs from Vermont since Alaska maintained its licensing scheme so that Alaskan residents were able to apply for concealed carry permits for reciprocity purposes with other states that require carry permits. Alaska also maintained the prohibition of concealed carry for anyone who was not permitted to carry a firearm under state or federal law.
- 2003: Minnesota and Colorado converted from "may issue" to "shall issue." Missouri and New Mexico converted from "no issue" to "shall issue."
- 2004: Ohio converted from "no issue" to "shall issue."
- 2006 Kansas and Nebraska converted from "no issue" to "shall issue."

By the end of the second wave of concealed carry licensing change, only Illinois and Wisconsin were left with "no issue" laws for concealed carry. The tally now stood as follows:

- 37 "shall issue" states.
- 9 "may issue" states.
- 2 "no issue" states.
- 2 unrestricted states.

Heller and Constitutional Carry

As previously mentioned, the 2008 case of District of Columbia v. Heller was a landmark case that changed the face of the Supreme Court's definition of the 2nd Amendment in relation to self-defense. It was ruled that the 2nd Amendment didn't just cover the right of the people to keep and bear arms so that they could partake in a well-organized militia. The ruling encompassed individuals who keep and bear arms for their individual self-defense.

From 2008 onwards, various other states have gone on to adopt policies for constitutional carry and the final two "no-issue" states caved in under the mounting pressure for a change in their laws.

- 2010: Arizona adopted constitutional carry.
- 2011: Wyoming adopted constitutional carry and Wisconsin converted from "no issue" to "shall issue", leaving only Illinois as the sole "no issue" hold out at the time. Iowa converted from "may issue" to "shall issue."
- 2013: Amidst ambiguity, Arkansas adopted constitutional carry. However, in 2018 the position was made concrete in the case of Taff v. State of Arkansas. During this case, an individual suspected of robbing a convenience store was found to be carrying a concealed firearm when interviewed. They were charged with unlawful carry which was later dismissed. Why? It was determined that the defendant had neither unlawfully used the firearm nor shown any intent of using it. The ruling was that a person that is not otherwise prohibited from carrying a firearm is not committing a criminal offense by simply carrying one.
- 2013: Illinois, the final "no issue" hold out, converted to "shall issue."
- 2015: Kansas and Maine adopted constitutional carry.
- 2016: Idaho, Mississippi, Missouri, West Virginia adopted a form of constitutional carry.
- 2017: New Hampshire and North Dakota adopted constitutional carry.
- January 31, 2019: South Dakota governor, Kristi Noem, went on to sign a bill into the law that converted the state to constitutional carry.

- 2018: Oklahoma passed a constitutional carry legislature which was turned down by Mary Fallin, the governor at the time. The new Oklahoma governor agreed to pass constitutional carry legislation providing it was sent to him.
- All states of America are either "may issue" or "shall issue", however, there are some locations that still practice "no issue."
- Hawaii is a "shall issue" state. The permit must be renewed annually. Only four permits have been issued since 1997, painting a picture of great difficulty acquiring a concealed carry permit in that state. The concealed carry permits from Hawaii are only valid in the country of issue, meaning that you can only carry in your home country.
- California and Rhode Island require applicants to apply at a local police agency. Some of these agencies are relatively liberal while others are incredibly strict and rarely grant any permits.
- Maryland, Massachusetts, New Jersey, New York, and New York City fall under the "may issue" category but are also known to be notoriously strict and reluctant in issuing permits.

January 2019: The Supreme Court issued a writ of certiorari in relation to New York City's restrictive concealed carry laws. A writ of certiorari is an instance where a lower court is ordered to present their records for a case so that the Supreme Court may review it.

Chapter 3:

Gun Ownership and Concealed Carry

vs. Open Carry

Gun ownership is a big decision that must be made logically and responsibly rather than in haste or on impulse. Both the benefits and risks must be taken into account and weighed to make the best decision.

Gun Ownership and Gun Control

Gun ownership is one of the most fervently debated and contentious social and political topics out there in modern America. On the one side of the fence, you have anti-gun lobbyists who fight for tighter gun control restrictions and put forward some very good reasoning behind their arguments. On the other side, you have gun owners who advocate the right and freedom of choice to be a responsible gun owner. The important word there is responsible. Irresponsible gun ownership puts the debate favorably in the hands of those who are anti-gun. Let's take a closer look at some arguments surrounding gun control.

Gun Control

Mass Shootings and Legally Purchased Firearms

The American magazine publication, *Mother Jones*, did a review of more than 70 cases of mass shootings that occurred over a period spanning more than 30 years. What they discovered, when they reviewed the incidents, is that almost 75% of those shootings were conducted using firearms that were legally purchased. This statistic proves that tighter gun control restrictions would bring the number of mass shooting incidents and killings down.

Access and Increased Risk of Violence

Linda Dahlberg conducted a study in 2004 in which she discovered that merely having a gun in your home inherently increases the risk of violent acts, such as suicide and homicide. The risk is there whether you own one or multiple guns, whether they are locked away safely or not. Arthur Kellerman published a study in the *New England Journal of Medicine*, proving that those living in a home that has a gun in it faced a risk of homicide 40 times greater than those living in a gun-free home. The risk of suicide by means of a firearm is 90 times greater when a firearm is present in the home. These statistics show that fewer guns in American homes would considerably decrease the risk of violence.

Prohibited Persons Owning Firearms

Under federal and state laws, certain persons are prohibited from owning and carrying a firearm. These individuals include convicted felons, for example. Background checks are required when purchasing firearms from licensed dealers but there is a loophole. Private gun sales are not required to perform background checks as long as the seller doesn't know or have a reasonable indication to believe that the buyer is prohibited from owning a firearm. There are 18 states that are an exception, and tighter gun control across the board could help prevent prohibited persons from owning guns.

Reasonable Firearm Control

Better gun control doesn't have to involve confiscating already purchased firearms or unreasonable restrictions. Various states across America don't require a permit for the purchase of a gun. By bringing in licensing and proof of eligibility, firearm safety could be increased. Eligibility may include having an understanding of the safe use and proficiency in handling a gun and could be proven through taking a certified training course.

Accidental Injuries and Deaths

Unintentional or accidental shootings account for a number of injuries and deaths. Many of these are attributed to unsafe handling and improper storage. Irresponsible gun ownership is the most dangerous aspect of a gun. A gun cannot discharge of its own accord; somebody has to be handling it for it to fire. If that person doesn't follow safe and responsible gun handling principles, it becomes a dangerous situation. Legislature for licensing and proof of proficiency in safe gun handling and storage regulations could see a decrease in accidental shootings.

Tighter Control and a Black Market

It's been proven that simply putting a law in place doesn't stop someone from acquiring something they really want. In fact, there is a possibility that tight restrictions could lead to the formation of a firearms black market for not only firearms, themselves, but also forged legal paperwork for permits, etc.

Guns and Crime

While it is arguable that gun control laws have seen a decrease in gun violence across the globe. However, a criminal will be a criminal irrespective of whether they are armed with a gun or not. If a gun is not available, other deadly weapons could be employed to conduct criminal activity. Such weapons may include bladed weapons, using a vehicle as a deadly weapon, and even homemade explosive devices.

Guns and Suicide

When you think about gun-related deaths, your immediate response is probably to think 'homicide'. This is actually not true. The majority of deaths in the United States involving a gun are suicide and not homicide. Fewer guns due to tighter restrictions will lower the statistics of gun-related deaths but won't change the fact that deaths due to other means will increase. If someone wants to commit suicide, not having a gun at hand isn't going to stop them. In this case, gun control isn't the answer, an increase in mental health services and support for individuals with mental illnesses or who are struggling with life would be more effective at saving lives.

Pros and Cons of Gun Ownership

There is only one real negative to owning and carrying a gun but it's something that needs careful consideration when deciding to bring a gun into your home and life. Guns are dangerous. They are deadly weapons that increase the risk of violence, injury, and death. Even if the firearm is kept for defensive purposes, a home with a gun in it is generally a more dangerous place than a home without a gun in it. As a responsible gun owner, you take that into consideration and do everything within your power to make having a gun in the home as safe as you possibly can.

That being said, there are a few pros to gun ownership. One benefit is the sense of security and the ability to protect yourself in a self-defense situation. Other pros include being able to partake in gun sports for pleasure or competition, and also being able to hunt for meat or pleasure. Gun ownership doesn't necessarily have to be for defensive purposes, either. Firearms collectors take great pride and pleasure in building their gun collections as a hobby. Now, you may think that gun collecting is a safe hobby and that you never have to shoot a gun if you are simply collecting them but this would be a misconception. Many gun collectors will routinely maintain and test fire their guns to make sure that they are still in working order. A vintage gun in working order is more valuable than one that is operational.

Concealed Carry vs. Open Carry

If you've decided to invest in a firearm for defensive purposes, you'll need to consider whether you want to carry the weapon openly or concealed. The debate about open versus concealed carry is an endless debate and gun owners often get into quite heated arguments about why their personal preference is the best. To decide which way of carrying is best suited for you can be difficult as there is a lot of contradicting information available. The best way to determine what you need, personally, is to educate yourself on all the pros and cons of both concealed and open carry to enable you to make a logical decision.

Definitions

- In the context of firearms, carrying means that you keep your gun readily accessible on your person. Usually, guns are carried in a holster or a sling as you go about your daily life.

- Open carry, in the United States, refers to openly carrying a firearm in public. The firearm is visible and not hidden under clothing or in any other way concealed from sight.
- Concealed carry is the opposite of open carry. You are carrying your weapon on your person or nearby, such as in a bag, and it is not visible to the casual observer.

Concealed carry has gotten a bad reputation due to criminal activity. Law-abiding citizens more readily openly carry their weapons because they have nothing to hide. Individuals with criminal intent, on the other hand, don't want to announce that intent or make themself conspicuous. The lawless throughout American history have favored concealing their weapons, a practice that is still in place today in the criminal element of society. Not only can they go about their devious activities without arousing suspicion, but they are also able to more easily catch their victims by surprise. The association of concealed carry with the intent of wrongdoing is transferred to even the most law-abiding citizens who practice concealed carry. People simply don't trust your intent because concealing your weapon automatically gives them the impression that you have something you feel the need to hide.

Pros and Cons

Both concealed and open carry each have pros and cons which need to be weighed up when deciding whether you are going to carry your firearm openly or conceal it on your person.

Deterrent

Open carry has the benefit of deterring would-be criminals or attackers. Someone who intends to do you harm will likely think twice if they can see that you are armed and in a position to defend yourself, especially if they, themselves, aren't armed with a deadly weapon. Even if a perpetrator is armed with a knife or gun, the knowledge that they are about to take on someone who is equally armed is a deterrent.

Concealing your weapon, however, doesn't give anybody else a clear indication that you are armed and capable of fighting back, putting you in a position of being more susceptible to someone initiating aggression as there is no visible deterrent.

Element of Surprise

While open carry can be seen as a deterrent to potential attacks, it can also give your attacker an advantage. They are aware that you are armed and can plan their attack in such a way that offers them the best opportunity of gaining the upper hand. Take into account that criminals tend to conceal their weapons, you are not likely to know they are armed, giving them the element of surprise. Concealed carry gives you the advantage of surprise as well in a defensive situation. Your attacker may not be prepared for your reaction to the threat and might be caught off guard when you draw your weapon.

Draw Time

In the battle of open versus concealed carry, open carry wins in the contest of draw time, hands down. It is quicker to draw from an openly visible and easily accessible holster than it is to fumble around underneath your clothing for a concealed weapon. Even if you are proficient at drawing a concealed weapon quickly, it still won't be as fast as if you were carrying it openly. The lag in draw time may not be huge but it may be enough to cost you your life in a self-defense situation.

Attention

Open carry comes with its fair share of attention. You are, after all, carrying a deadly weapon that inherently draws the attention of others. This is neither particularly good nor bad. In the sense that the weapon could act as a visible deterrent, it's not a bad thing in the least. However, you could attract unwanted negative attention due to the potential prejudice some may have toward guns. You may also end up being roped into an unwelcome conversation about guns and gun control or become the subject of open criticism. Concealing your weapon leaves those around you are none the wiser. Nobody will give you a second look, voice their criticism, or in any other way pay any more attention to you than normal.

Awareness

Concealed carry brings no public attention to gun ownership at all, unless, of course, a concealed weapon is used to commit a criminal offense. Open carry brings attention to gun ownership and raises awareness about responsible gun ownership and open carry laws.

Intimidation

Openly carrying a deadly weapon on your belt may immediately intimidate those around you the moment they lay eyes on you and your visibly gun. Deadly weapons tend to instill fear in people, especially with the prevalence of gun violence in criminal activity. An intimidated and fearful bystander may be clueless as to the state's open carry gun laws and call law enforcement out of concern. While law enforcement may relay the laws to that bystander, if the bystander doesn't communicate the situation effectively, you could be facing the boys in blue. If that were to happen, good communication on your behalf would be essential to handle the situation correctly and avoid being shot by the police. Concealed carry wouldn't intimidate or scare anybody or raise suspicion.

Easy Target

Open carry may act as a deterrent but it could also make your firearm an easy target for an attacker, even if the attacker isn't armed. Being confident in your firearm acting as a deterrent could lead you to neglect learning hand-to-hand combat skills and gun retention. Gun retention is the ability to keep hold of your gun when someone is trying to wrestle it out of your holster or away from you. Being shot with your own gun is never a desired outcome. When carrying your firearm concealed, there is no weapon visible for an attacker to target. Not only might an attacker target your weapon, but they may also actually target you. In a defense situation where an attacker is armed and faced with two victims, they may target the visibly armed victim first as opposed to the victim who is carrying a concealed weapon. The intent in doing so is to eliminate the most obvious opposition to their attack and remove the threat to the attacker themself.

The Law

While all 50 states have laws in place permitting concealed carry, only 31 states allow open carry. Most states permitting concealed carry require a permit to do so but, providing you are in possession of a permit, no states prohibit concealed carry altogether.

Comfort

Concealing a weapon may not be the most comfortable way to carry it. You have to hide the weapon if carrying it on your person, which means that it will likely be carried underneath clothing. Having a firearm pressed up against your body while you move may not always be pleasant. When you carry openly, you can wear a holster outside your clothing which may ultimately be more comfortable.

What to Choose?

Whether you choose concealed carry or open carry will depend, firstly, on the laws in your state or jurisdiction. Secondly, it will come down to personal preference. Can you handle unwanted conversation or criticism? Do you mind authorities giving you flack or keeping a closer eye on you when you're out and about? Do you mind the extra attention your open carry would draw? Do you mind raising suspicion among authorities and the public, alike, by carrying a concealed weapon? You need to weigh up each of the pros and cons to both open and concealed carry and carefully make your decision based on what you, personally, would prefer.

Chapter 4:

Carrying: Legal Considerations

Owning and carrying a firearm is a big responsibility and comes with various legal considerations. Even if your state doesn't require a license to carry, you should still consider aspects, such as legal insurance, knowing your state laws or the laws of any states you visit, and prohibited venues. Licensing will often be your first port of call.

Firearm Licensing

A gun license is a license or permit that is issued to individuals by a government authority, such as the police, within a jurisdiction. The license authorizes the individual to purchase, own, possess, or to carry a firearm. These permits are issued subject to various conditions or even some restrictions. Often the conditions involve appropriate storage as dictated by the jurisdiction or taking a gun safety training course to ensure that you are knowledgeable about handling firearms in a safe, responsible way. One of the more serious conditions and restrictions involved in licensing is having a background check performed. The government prohibits certain individuals from owning and carrying a firearm and police will want to make sure that you are permitted, by law, to get a license. In addition to purchasing the firearm itself, permits may be necessary to purchase ammunition.

The scope of the license will depend on the firearm you want to purchase and what you intend to do with it. There are some jurisdictions that might require a license to own a gun, a license to use it for hunting, or a license to carry the firearm concealed. You may even be required to have different firearm licenses for different types of guns if you own more than one type, such as handguns and shotguns. Laws regarding licensing will vary from state to state and whether you can carry a firearm from one state into another will depend on the reciprocity laws between states.

Important Note: It is vitally important to always check the firearm licensing laws for the jurisdiction you are in and to keep up-to-date with any changes made to the laws, nationally or at the state level.

Who Can Get a License?

- Persons who are citizens of the United States.
- Individuals who are nationals of the United States but not citizens.
- Permanent residents who are in the United States lawfully – often referred to as "green card" holders.
- Lawfully admitted aliens to the United States who have been admitted under a non-immigrant visa providing that alien falls into one of these exceptions:
  - Lawful sporting or hunting purposes.
  - Possession of a lawful hunting license that has been issued by any state in the United States.
  - Official foreign government representative accredited to the United States Government or accredited to an international organization headquartered in the United States or is traveling to another country where they are accredited.
  - Department of State designated distinguished foreign visitors or foreign government officials.
  - Foreign officer in law enforcement from a friendly foreign government traveling into the United States on official business relating to law enforcement.

- A waiver has been issued by the United States Attorney General providing the waiver petition proves that it's both in the interest of justice and does not put public safety at risk under 18 U.S. Code § 922(y)(3)(c).
- Important Note: Each state will have its own regulations and laws pertaining to individuals eligible to own a firearm.

Who Can't Get a License?

Individuals who fall under any of the following categories are not permitted, under the 1968 Gun Control Act, to either, transport, ship, receive, or possess any firearms or ammunition.

- Fugitives from the law.
- Individuals with convictions from any court related to a crime that is punishable by imprisonment for a period of longer than one year.
- Individuals under indictment related to a crime that is punishable by imprisonment for a period of longer than one year.
- Any individual who unlawfully uses or is addicted to any controlled substance
- Persons with adjudications of defective mental ability or who have been committed to a mental institution.
- Undocumented immigrants—also known as illegal aliens.
- Individuals who have been dishonorably discharged from the Armed Forces.
- Persons who've renounced their nationality or citizenship of the United States.
- Individuals who have a restraining order against them to prevent harassment, stalking, or threatening of an intimate partner or that partner's child.

- Persons who've been convicted of a domestic violence misdemeanor crime.

Important note: This is not an exhaustive list of prohibited persons. Always check with the national and state regulations regarding who can and cannot own or possess a firearm.

Concealed Carry Licensing Requirements

In those states where a concealed carry license is required in order to carry your weapon concealed, to apply and successfully obtain a license, you will need to meet certain criteria. Some states may require applicants to verify that they are proficient in firearm handling, usually having undergone some sort of certified training. There are some training courses created by the National Rifle Association that make use of combined live-fire instruction and classroom education which generally meet the training requirements. Some states recognize your military or police service training (if you are or have been part of the Armed Forces or law enforcement) as suitable training to meet the requirements.

Classroom education for firearms training usually includes:
- Firearm operations and terminology.
- How to clean and maintain a firearm.
- Methods for carrying and safety.
- Liability concerns.
- Concealed carry limitations and legislature.
- Home or self-defense.
- How to diffuse a confrontational situation.
- Gun handling techniques practice without firing the gun.

Some states may require a training course to include a practical element in order to meet the training requirements. During these practical lessons, the trainee fires the weapon as a way to demonstrate safe handling and operating a gun and how to shoot accurately at distances common in self-defense situations.

You can typically complete a concealed carry training course in one day and that certification is viable for a set period of time. How long training course certifications are valid will depend on individual state regulations.

Each state that allows concealed carry has state-specific concealed carry licensing requirements that an applicant needs to meet in order to be granted a permit. Check your local and state laws to make sure that you, as a license applicant, meet the requirements. You can apply for a license at a police station in your jurisdiction. If you are unclear about any state-specific concealed carry requirements, consult a lawyer or law enforcement for advice. Once granted, the license will typically be valid for a specific period of time, after that time period it will need to be renewed, much like vehicle licenses. When renewing a concealed carry license, you may need to go for training certification again.

Legal Insurance

As part of being a responsible gun owner who carries a concealed weapon, legal insurance is a no-brainer. You never know where or when you may need to draw and fire your weapon. All instances of using a firearm come with risk and consequence, even in self-defense situations.

What are the implications of using a firearm in self-defense?
- Cost of posting bail.
- Confiscation of weapons.
- Income loss.
- Several court appearances.
- Legal services retention costs.

- Damages as a result of civil litigation ending in unfavorable judgment.

Why Is Concealed Carry Insurance Important?

Concealed carry insurance is also referred to as CCW and firearm liability insurance. It is an affordable coverage offering legal protection if you find yourself in a situation in which you have no choice but to use your gun against an attacker. Many types of firearm legal insurance coverage also help protect you in the case of being hit with a lawsuit filed by a party involved in an incident.

How Does it Work?

Both the type and the level of coverage will depend on the policy and the limits you choose to set for the policy. For some policies, a provider will offer upfront payment for legal defense after a self-defense shooting. Other policies and providers will only offer compensation when the case has been resolved. The amount of coverage also varies greatly according to policy and provider.

Depending on the policy you choose and the provider you are insured with, policies may cover aspects such as a loss or interruption of income, bail funds, attorney retainer fees, replacement of a firearm, and others.

If you find yourself in a situation of a self-defense shooting, even if your actions are justifiable and the outcome favorable, there are heavy costs involved. If you are not covered by a form of legal insurance, you stand to lose a lot, even if you manage to save your life or the life of someone you love. Responsible gun ownership takes all the aspects of owning a deadly weapon into account. As a responsible gun owner, you cannot afford to own and carry a firearm without having the backing of legal insurance.

Restricted Premises for Firearms

A concealed carry license allows the holder of that license to carry a concealed weapon in public. However, that doesn't mean to say that you can carry your firearm absolutely anywhere and everywhere. There are several generally accepted premises where you cannot carry a firearm, open or concealed, as a civilian, even if the premises are open to the public.

Federal Government Facilities

- IRS offices.
- Post offices.
- Military/VA facilities.
- Federal court buildings.
- Correctional facilities.
- Corps of Engineers-controlled property.
- Amtrak facilities and trains.

Bureau of Land Management Premises

Carrying a firearm on land that is controlled by the Bureau of Land Management (including areas such as federal parks and wildlife preservation areas):

- Permitted by federal law under the 2009 CARD Act but individual state laws still apply so it is a good idea to check and confirm your local laws.
- While carrying is permitted, it is prohibited in structures, buildings, and restrooms in federal parks even if concealed carry may be permitted in these parks provided that you have a

permit that is recognized by the state in which the federal park is located.

- Carrying a concealed firearm into caves located in federal parks is prohibited.

State and Local Government Facilities

- DMV and DoT offices.
- Courthouses.
- Correctional facilities.
- Police stations.
- Places where government entities meet (with some exceptions for certain individuals working in such places which may include judges, government officials, lawyers).

Venues for Political Events

- Parades rallies.
- Polling locations.
- Debates.

Educational Facilities

- Elementary schools.
- Secondary schools.
- Colleges.
- Universities.

Some states may offer "drop-off exceptions" in which only carrying a firearm inside the educational facility's buildings is prohibited. Some states may provide a permit to carry a firearm when inside your personal vehicle while on school property. Carry laws for campuses vary by state, be sure to check your local laws.

Entertainment Facilities

- Public sporting events and sporting event venues.
- Fairs.
- Amusement parks.
- Carnivals.
- Parades.

Alcohol-Trading Businesses

- Restaurants.
- Bars.
- Nightclubs.
- Sometimes any establishment where the percentage of the total trade sales from selling alcohol is above a certain amount.

Medical Facilities

- Hospitals.
- Even if a hospital isn't restricted it may be partnered with a medical school for educational purposes and then is considered an educational facility as listed above.
- The exception to the prohibited carry of firearms in hospitals may be medical professionals working within the facility. This may vary by state or even by facility.

Places of Worship

- Churches.
- Synagogues.
- Mosques.
- Temples.
- Any place that is considered a place or house of worship.

Transport

- Municipal transport facilities and vehicles that transport a large amount of people such as trains.
- Airport sterile areas; these are often areas of the airport situated past security screening checkpoints and are often only accessible to authorized persons.
- Carrying is prohibited on a ship or aircraft unless authorized by the captain of the ship or the pilot of the aircraft.

Non-Government Facilities With Elevated Security Precautions

- Facilities producing oil and gas.
- Power plants.
- Nuclear facilities.
- Dams.
- Factories.
- Banks.

Private Property

All privately owned property where the lawful owner or tenant has verbally stated or posted a sign prohibiting the carry of firearms on the premises

Under the Influence

- Carrying is prohibited in any public place while the gun handler is under the influence of alcohol or narcotics.
- Included are some over-the-counter (OTC) and prescription medications but varies according to local jurisdiction.

Gun-Free Areas

- Certain states permit private businesses to post signs that prohibit the carrying of a concealed weapon while on the premises.
- The sign's format and language varies according to state.
- Such signs carry the same restrictive regulations as those pertaining to schools and hospitals.
- In some states failing to comply with these signs may result in your concealed carry permit being revoked and criminal charges being laid.
- In some states failing to comply with these signs is treated as violating a trespassing law.
- Laws and repercussions vary according to state.

There is controversy and debate over gun-free areas as it is only law-abiding citizens who willingly adhere to the regulation. Individuals or groups with criminal intent will not adhere to the signage. Furthermore, there a is debate over whether individuals or groups intent on committing mass murder may specifically seek out gun-free areas such as schools and malls as the people inside will be disarmed and unable to fight back or protect themselves.

Concealed Carry: Printing and Brandishing

Printing is where a concealed weapon is visible underneath clothing, often by shape or outline, but the firearm is still fully covered by the material.

Brandishing may refer to openly displaying a concealed carry weapon or printing. Brandishing by openly displaying the weapon may refer to pulling clothing back to reveal the gun or unholstering the firearm and displaying it in your hand. Brandishing is considered a crime in many jurisdictions but the definition of what constitutes brandishing varies from one jurisdiction to the next.

Dealing With Law Enforcement and Traffic Stops

Sometimes it can be easy to overlook knowing how to deal with law enforcement when you are carrying a weapon in your vehicle. After all, you have a legal license or permit, you're an upstanding citizen, and you practice safe and responsible gun ownership and handling principles. However, law enforcement officers aren't mind readers and psychics who know and see all. They can't tell who the good or bad guys are without investigating the situation further. You throw an uncertain officer of the law and a concealed firearm into the same situation and the chances of it turning sour are greatly increased unless you are prepared to handle the encounter before it even arises.

Even the most law-abiding citizen can make a mistake and be stopped by the police. Perhaps your license plate fell off without you noticing it. Perhaps you accidentally ran a stop sign because you were distracted.

Perhaps you have a broken tail light of which you weren't aware. Maybe you just find yourself being pulled over at a routine roadblock. The possibilities are endless and you need to know how to deal with the situation calmly and correctly to avoid any misunderstandings that could see you in handcuffs.

- When a police officer flashes his lights behind you as an indication of pulling you over, immediately acknowledge the signal by turning on the appropriate signal indicator to tell them that you are pulling off the road. Even if it takes you a few moments to be able to safely pull off, slowing down and signaling indicates your intent to comply.

- Once safely pulled over to a stop, switch your vehicle's ignition off, this tells police that you don't intend to speed away at the first chance.

- If stopped at night, switch on the vehicle's interior lights, allowing law enforcement a better assessment of the inside of your vehicle and any passengers. When police can better assess the situation, they can feel more at ease when they observe that the situation isn't threatening in any way because you are making an effort to show that you have nothing to hide.

- As law enforcement approaches, don't fumble around inside the car or glove box. This kind of movement, from a distance, makes it appear that you are either trying to hide something or reach for a weapon. If you keep your legal paperwork in your vehicle, such as insurance, licensing, and registration, keep them in an easily accessible place so that you don't have to fumble around.

- If possible, open both the driver and passenger side windows in the front of the vehicle and place your hands on the top of your steering wheel, in plain sight and relaxed.

- If the officer requests your ID, registration, or any other paperwork, clearly tell them where those items are before you reach for them. Being open and honest gives the officer an indication that you are one of the good guys and that you want to comply safely.

- Once you have handed your license and concealed carry permit to the officer, place your hands back on the top of the steering wheel.
- If asked whether you are actually carrying a firearm with you at that time, keep your hands on the steering wheel and tell the officer where your firearm is in the vehicle.
- Many states allow law enforcement a reasonable amount of leeway for making a judgment on how to handle you and your gun while performing a traffic stop. The firearm may be left where it is with your hands still visible on the steering wheel. You may be requested to hand over your firearm. You may be requested to exit the vehicle and allow the officer to remove the firearm themself.
- Providing that you are not wanted by the law, that the firearm hasn't been used in a crime or been reported stolen, and that this is simply a routine traffic stop, there should be no problem. The officer has the discretion to handle the situation in the best possible way to ensure their own safety, the safety of others, and your safety. Your firearm should be returned to you without fuss once the contact has ended.
- Do not begin to argue with law enforcement at any point during the contact. If they would like to inspect the firearm or remove it and place it in a safe location until it is returned to you, allow it to happen. If you feel that your rights are being violated in a significant way, it's best to let things play out and then consult your attorney afterward.

Several states don't require an individual with a legal permit to carry a weapon, open or concealed, to provide law enforcement with that license or to reveal that they are armed. If the state you are in does not require you to hand over your license or inform the officer that you are armed, you may want to do so anyway. If it is suddenly discovered that you are carrying a concealed defensive weapon, the situation could escalate unpleasantly. Perhaps the wind blows your shirt hem up and it becomes visible or the officer catches a glimpse of the weapon while you are retrieving your vehicle registration from the glove box.

Never underestimate the power of courtesy, honesty, and transparency when dealing with law enforcement. Use good manners; be willing to comply. It may not get you out of getting a ticket for a traffic violation, but it will go a long way to keeping the situation as calm as possible.

Know the Law

It cannot be stated enough that a good knowledge of local and state laws regarding carrying a defensive weapon, especially when carrying concealed, is vital. If you are carrying a weapon over state lines, be sure about the reciprocity of the states you are traveling to, and the local and state laws within the jurisdictions you will be visiting. Ignorance of the law isn't a defense in court and ignorance of the law could land you in a lot of hot water unnecessarily. It is also important to regularly check the laws to ensure that you don't miss any amendments or new laws.

Chapter 5:

The Use of Deadly Force

You have probably heard the phrase "use of deadly force" many times before but do you have a clear comprehension of what it means in terms of the law? When you are a gun owner, it is important to understand what deadly force is, how it relates to firearm use, and how it affects you.

Defining Deadly Force

Deadly force may also be called lethal force. It refers to using force that will probably cause grievous bodily injury or even death to a person. In most cases, the only justification for the use of deadly force is when it is used as a last resort in instances of extreme need. You must have exhausted all your other options of lesser use of force before resorting to lethal force for that action to later be considered justified.

Traditional weapons that account for use of deadly force when employed include, but are not limited to:

- Bladed weapons.
- Firearms.
- Vehicles.
- Explosives.

Non-Traditional weapons that account for use of deadly force when employed include, but are not limited to:

- Sharp objects.
- Baseball bat.
- Pieces of wood.
- Tire iron.
- Bricks.

As you can see, weapons that may account for deadly force could vary greatly. Sometimes the normal use of the weapon, itself, presents a deadly force, as is the case with bladed weapons and firearms. In other instances, it is how the weapon is used, how much force is applied, and how badly the person is injured, as is the case with a baseball bat or a brick. This makes defining the use of deadly force a delicate and oftentimes complicated subject. In most cases, you can judge whether the force is deadly or not by how much force is put behind the weapon and how badly the person is injured.

Example: You could pick up a piece of firewood and take a medium-force swipe at someone, injuring them but not seriously. This wouldn't be considered the use of deadly force. On the other hand, you could put all your strength behind the swing, strike someone in the head and crack their skull, put them in a coma, or even fatally wound them. In that instance, it would be considered the use of deadly force. What you then need to consider is whether the situation warranted the use of deadly force.

Stand Your Ground Law

The stand your ground law is also sometimes referred to as the no duty to retreat law or the line in the sane law. This law allows an individual to use deadly force when they believe, without reasonable doubt, that it is necessary for them to defend themselves against the threat of grievous bodily injury, kidnapping, rape, or death. In some jurisdictions, robbery may be included, as well as some other serious crimes, in which an individual has a right to self-defense. Under the stand your ground law, an individual does not have the duty of retreating before they employ the use of deadly force in a self-defense situation. However, this is only applicable if the individual using deadly force to defend themself is doing so in a location in which they are lawfully present. You cannot cite the stand your ground law for employing the use of deadly force in self-defense if you are unlawfully present in the location. You may also not invoke the stand your ground law in self-defense if you are making the first aggressive move in a situation of confrontation or if you are engaged in any form of criminal activity. The exact details about when and under what circumstances you can and cannot invoke the stand your ground law varies by jurisdiction. It is important to research and be informed about the particular ins and outs of the law for the area in which you live.

Stand Your Ground and Racial Disparity

Considering the racial disparity, or the racial difference, in relation to early concealed carry laws, one might expect to find a difference in prosecution rates and success between African-Americans and Caucasians. However, this isn't the case in recent times. It seems that equality and fairness in the eyes of the law regarding standing your ground is victorious.

In 2012, the case of Trayvon Martin caused widespread ripples regarding the stand your ground and self-defense laws. In this case, 17-year-old Trayvon Martin, a high school student of African-American descent, was visiting relatives in a gated community on the 26th of February, 2012. George Zimmerman, a 28-year-old neighborhood watchman of mixed race, alleged a confrontation with Trayvon. It is alleged that Zimmerman shot the unarmed Trayvon, killing him, and was injured in the confrontation. Zimmerman claimed self-defense. He was charged with a count of murder for the shooting death of Trayvon. However, Zimmerman claimed self-defense in the confrontation at trial and was subsequently acquitted. The Department of Justice reviewed the case for any possible civil rights infringements but no additional charges were filed due to insufficient evidence.

Reacting to the widely publicized Trayvon Martin case, the Tampa Bay Times went about putting together a report on how the stand your ground laws are applied. They compiled a database of cases wherein the defendants invoked or tried to invoke the stand your ground law in self-defense. What they found was that, within Florida, there was no racial disparity in the prosecution of cases wherein the defendants claimed their actions were in self-defense under the law. Both Caucasian and African-American individuals were being both charged and convicted at similar rates. However, it was found that victims of African-American attackers more successfully applied and used the stand your ground law in self-defense than the victims of Caucasian attackers irrespective of the race of the victim. What this means is that whether the victim was Caucasian or African-American, if the attacks were made by an African-American, the law was more successfully applied and used than if the attacker was Caucasian. Does this equate to racial prejudice regarding the ethnicity of the attacker? That is not a given. It was determined that the probability of African-American attackers being armed was higher and so was the likelihood of such attackers to be involved in committing crimes, such as robbery or burglary, at the time of the attack.

Stand Your Ground Controversy

Opposition and anti-gun activists and groups frequently label stand your ground laws as "shoot first, ask questions later". Before the enactment of Florida's stand your ground law; John F. Timoney, then Miami chief of police, stated that "whether it's trick-or-treaters or kids playing in the yard of someone who doesn't want them there or some drunk guy stumbling into the wrong house, you're encouraging people to possibly use deadly physical force where it shouldn't be used." (Wikipedia, 2020) To a certain degree, the argument holds water as there are those individuals who will seek to invoke the law whilst involved in committing a crime and the enactment of the law potentially makes it more difficult to prosecute such individuals successfully. However, on the flip side of the coin, there is an argument that the duty to retreat law puts the safety of the criminal above the life and safety of the victim. In real life-threatening circumstances, having to exhaust all other avenues of defense or having to focus on safe retreat instead of self-defense could mean the difference between living and dying.

Not only is the stand your ground law subject to debated controversy, it was actually found to be confusing. A task force was appointed by Fort Lauderdale's State Sen. Chris Smith to conduct an investigation. The investigation determined that the law was not easy for the general public to understand and that it could easily be misconstrued in the face of a threat. If the public is not completely conversant of the law and don't comprehend it fully, it leaves individuals vulnerable to making judgment mistakes which could cause unnecessarily loss of life. Part of the supporting evidence that the law was confusing and dangerous was the outcome of the Trayvon Martin case in which George Zimmernam was acquitted. The suggestion was made, by a representative of the Florida Prosecuting Attorneys Association, Buddy Jacobs, that the law should actually be scrapped. Obviously, anti-gun lobbyists backed this suggestion as it would help curb the potential of unnecessary shootings. In a speech on the 16th of July, 2013, Eric Holder, Attorney General, further picked the stand your ground law apart, stating that the law, as it stands, is "senselessly expanding the concept of self-defense and sowing dangerous conflict in our neighborhoods." (Wikipedia, 2020)

However, as with any dark cloud, there is a silver lining in this controversy over the stand your ground law. In a very interesting turn of events, George Zimmerman, himself, alleged that he was restrained when the shooting happened. He stated that he would not have been able to safely retreat because of being restrained and, therefore, the stand your ground law was irrelevant in his case.

2014: Florida considered changing the law to include a bill that would allow individuals the opportunity to display a firearm or even fire a warning shot when in a confrontation. The aim was to lessen the likelihood of a prison sentence.

2017: A bill was proposed in Florida's legislature that would put the onus on the prosecution to provide proof whether self-defense by the defendant was not a valid option.

2018: The widely publicized case of the Markeis McGlockton shooting, six years after the Trayvon Martin incident, brought about a new debate concerning Florida's stand your ground law. In the case, 28-year-old Markeis McGlockton was shot and killed by Michael Drejka over a dispute about parking in a disabled parking zone without a placard. Drejka approached McGlockton's car before the shooting and started a verbal confrontation during which he pointed a finger at Britany Jacobs, McGlockton's girlfriend. The issue at hand was that the car was parked in a disabled parking zone without a visible permit. When McGlockton exited the store and observed the confrontation, he pushed Drejka to the ground. At this stage in the confrontation, Drejka drew his firearm and within two and a half seconds of hitting the ground, he shot McGlockton who subsequently died at a local hospital from the injuries sustained. At first, Drejka was not charged with the killing of McGlockton when the case was heard in the Pinellas County Sheriff's Office. The Sheriff, Bob Gualtieri, cited the stand your ground law as the reason for no charge. Subsequently, the case was investigated and turned over to Bernie McCabe, the Sixth Judicial Circuit Court of Florida State Attorney. McCabe charged Drejka with a count of manslaughter to which Drejka pleaded not guilty. Ultimately, Drejka was convicted of manslaughter and sentenced to 20 years imprisonment.

As you can see, there is much controversy surrounding stand your ground laws, Florida is but one example. The laws of gun control and sensible, responsible gun ownership rely on the citizens to take the responsibility for wielding a deadly weapon. It is each person's responsibility to themselves and those around them to remember the rules of responsible gun ownership and to always think with a clear head in both confrontational and even life-threatening circumstances. There are many who will argue that the law allows too much liberty. On the other hand, there are those who will argue that the liberty the law allows is due but it is up to the individual to use that liberty responsibly and weigh up all options before resorting to a drastic resolution. As the popular phrase says, "With great power comes great responsibility."

Duty to Retreat Law

The duty to retreat law is directly opposite to the stand your ground law. According to this law, you are required to safely retreat instead of fighting back when under threat of attack whenever it is possible to do so. You are only allowed to defend yourself with force if you do not have the option of a safe retreat and even then, it is your duty to prove that you had no other choice. Some American states employ stand your ground laws that don't include an aspect of the duty to retreat but rather grant an individual permission to match force for force when in confrontation, even if that means matching deadly force for deadly force.

While most jurisdictions across the United States employ a stand your ground law, there are several jurisdictions wherein a duty to retreat law is upheld. However, many states that do employ a duty to retreat law do so with special considerations to being in your own home, vehicle, or place of work. This is termed the castle doctrine.

Did you know: Historically, American law takes much of its inspiration from English law. At the time of importing the duty to retreat law, it was founded on English common law which required an individual to retreat when land or property was involved in a confrontation. The individual would then have to seek civil means of resolving the conflict instead of 'taking the law into their own hands'. In modern America, most states have clarified their laws regarding forcible entry, both civil and penal. This was done to remove the previous common law liberty to use force when recovering land or property.

Castle Doctrine

Also known as castle law, the castle doctrine is a legal doctrine that stems from the old adage that a man's home is his castle. It is a governing principle that is employed by many jurisdictions and it isn't an actual law that can be invoked. It isn't a get-out-of-jail-free card that you can play to provide yourself with immunity against prosecution in instances of the use of deadly force in one's own home. What it comes down to is that, if a jurisdiction has a castle doctrine, that jurisdiction simply applies a belief or principle to their proceedings when they are handling matters of law.

The castle doctrine is the belief that an individual who is faced with a situation "when the actor reasonably fears imminent peril of death or serious bodily harm to him or herself or another" (Wikipedia, 2020) is permitted to react with force. This principle is only applicable to one's own home or, in some jurisdictions, where they are legally present such as their own vehicle or place of work. The doctrine may provide a certain amount of protection and immunity in cases where force is used for self-defense but as it isn't a law, the protections and immunities aren't guaranteed.

The castle doctrine is not absolute and does not always trump the duty to retreat. An individual may still have a duty to retreat where it is possible in a bid to avoid the use of force. It does, however, reduce the duty to retreat when an individual is attacked within their own home.

The problem with the castle doctrine is that it is a principle that is not based on fact. Merely having a trespasser present and feeling fearful for your safety is enough to cite the castle doctrine. However, that does not take factual evidence into account. For instance; if a drunken man were to stumble mistakenly into your home, there is a trespasser present and you may be fearful for your safety. Using force against the drunken man is therefore justifiable under the principle of the castle doctrine. However, using deadly force that may result in the drunken man's death isn't automatically excusable under the castle doctrine. This is where things get a little bit sticky on the legal side of things.

The castle doctrine must not be misconstrued with justifiable homicide in self-defense. Homicide in self-defense due to a confrontation within one's own home is a completely different matter of law. Why? Generally speaking, to prove that homicide was justifiable, an individual must prove beyond all reasonable doubt that the intruder had it in mind to commit a felony or an act of violence. It is not enough to presume what the intruder was intending on doing and reacting out of fear. In the case of the drunken man stumbling into your home, killing him by shooting him with your firearm does not equate to justifiable homicide. There is no way to prove that the unarmed drunken man had the intent of violence or committing a crime against you. You would be up for criminal homicide and wrongful death. Even if the drunken man was armed, it must be proven beyond all reasonable doubt that his intent was to actively enter your home and commit a crime using that weapon. Otherwise, it is simply a case of an armed drunken man mistakenly stumbling into the wrong home with no intention of causing anyone any harm. Killing him would result in wrongful death and prosecution.

Let's clear up what the castle doctrine is and what it isn't:

- A castle doctrine isn't a law, it is only a principle or belief that is incorporated into many jurisdictions.
- A castle doctrine doesn't negate a duty to retreat; it may simply reduce the duty to retreat.
- A castle doctrine and justifiable homicide in self-defense are not one and the same thing.
- Citing a castle doctrine doesn't automatically make homicide in self-defense justifiable.
- Justifiable homicide in self-defense requires proof beyond a reasonable doubt that the person intended to commit a grievous act of violence toward you.

The castle doctrine and its use in the United States remain controversial. A notable controversial case in which the castle doctrine was invoked is the death of Yoshihiro Hattori in 1992. Yoshihiro Hattori was a Japanese exchange student who accidentally went to the wrong house on his way to a Halloween party in Baton Rouge, Louisiana. The homeowner assumed that Hattori was trespassing with criminal intent and fatally shot him.

A Brief Look at Laws by State

Stand Your Ground States

Thirty-five states support the stand your ground law, 27 of which have policies in place stating that an individual has no duty to retreat from an attack in a location where they are lawfully present. Ten of these states also include in their law "may stand your ground" language.

- Alabama—May stand your ground.
- Alaska.
- Arizona.
- Florida—May stand your ground.
- Georgia—May stand your ground.
- Idaho—May stand your ground.
- Indiana.
- Iowa.
- Kansas—May stand your ground.
- Kentucky—May stand your ground.
- Louisiana—May stand your ground.
- Michigan.
- Mississippi.
- Missouri.
- Montana.

- Nevada.
- New Hampshire.
- North Carolina.
- Oklahoma—May stand your ground.
- Pennsylvania—May stand your ground (No duty to retreat is limited to circumstances in which an individual is defending against an attacker with a deadly weapon.)
- South Carolina—May stand your ground.
- South Dakota.
- Tennessee.
- Texas.
- Utah.
- West Virginia.
- Wyoming.

Duty to Retreat States

- Arkansas.
- Connecticut—Not applicable in the defendant's place of work.
- Delaware—Not applicable in the defendant's place of work.
- Hawaii—Not applicable in the defendant's place of work.
- Maine.
- Maryland.
- Massachusetts.
- Minnesota.
- Nebraska—Not applicable in the defendant's place of work.
- New Jersey
- New York—Not applicable in cases of burglary, robbery, sexual assault, and kidnapping.
- North Dakota—Not applicable in the defendant's place of work.
- Ohio—Not applicable in the defendant's own vehicle.

- Rhode Island.
- Wisconsin—Not applicable in the defendant's own vehicle. Not applicable in the defendant's place of work but only if the defendant is the workplace's owner or operator.

In all states that require the duty to retreat, it is not applicable when the defending individual is in their own home. The exception is that some jurisdictions do not negate the duty to retreat when defending in one's own home when an individual is defending against another occupant of the same home, otherwise known as the castle doctrine.

Middle Ground

Washington D.C. approaches stand your ground and duty to retreat laws differently. A retreat is not required by law. However, it must be determined whether the individual had reason to believe they were in imminent danger at the time and that they had to use deadly force to defend themself. It must also be taken into consideration, incorporating other evidence, whether the individual did have the option of retreating safely but did not do so.

No Law

Both American Samoa and the United States Virgin Islands have no settled law on the subjects of stand your ground and duty to retreat.

Self-Defense in the United States

Self-defense, as a term, is pretty self-explanatory. It is the defense of oneself in the face of attack from another. However, what does that mean in terms of claiming self-defense when reciprocating the force from your attacker?

Self-defense, in the United States, is an affirmative defense that may be employed for the justification of using force against another person under certain circumstances. An affirmative defense is a little trickier to explain. An affirmative defense is one that can be factually proven and which negates legal prosecution for otherwise unlawful actions. A plaintiff or prosecutor alleges certain facts pertaining to a case. For an affirmative defense to work, the defendant must be able to prove a different fact that will rule out legal consequences of the illegal action the prosecutor or plaintiff is accusing the defendant of.

In terms of self-defense, having shot an intruder in your home requires the defendant to prove beyond a reasonable doubt that there was no other choice but to shoot the intruder. The plaintiff, or the intruder, may accuse the defendant of unlawfully shooting them or using an unreasonable amount of force. The onus would be on the defendant to successfully prove that they were left with absolutely no other choice and should it be proven, self-defense may be used as an affirmative defense.

In the United States, the general rule of self-defense states:

"A person is privileged to use such force as reasonably appears necessary to defend him or herself against an apparent threat of unlawful and immediate violence from another." (Wikipedia, 2020)

In instances where non-deadly force is involved, the defendant must have the reasonable belief that their use of force against the other person was essential to avoid approaching unlawful physical harm to themself. In instances where deadly force is used during a self-defense claim, the defendant must have the reasonable belief that immediate use of deadly force is essential to prevent the other person from inflicting grievous physical harm or even death upon them.

Imperfect Defense, Exceptions, Limitations

Someone who initiates aggression in a confrontation can't claim self-defense as a justification for their actions. The exceptions are when they stop the confrontation with clear verbal communication and are required to defend themselves from continued attack or if the other person responded with excessive force that is disproportionate to the force they were using.

In times gone by, an individual could claim self-defense when resisting unlawful arrest. However, recent times have seen a trend that moves away from the claim of self-defense for this purpose. These days, most jurisdictions that permit an individual to resist an unlawful arrest will require the use of excessive force during the arrest to justify the defendant's actions under a claim of self-defense.

Self-defense isn't always a viable option, even if an individual believes with full conviction that their actions were justified. This is what is known as an imperfect defense. The defendant whole-heartedly believes that their use of deadly force was justified when, in reality, it wasn't legally justified. In this instance, the defendant may have a murder charge reduced to a charge of manslaughter instead.

Self-Defense and Retreat

Many jurisdictions within the United States don't follow the common law principle of duty to retreat before resorting to using deadly force against a threat. In fact, many states employ the stand your ground rule, as previously mentioned, which negates the necessity to retreat at all. However, irrespective of whether a jurisdiction has a duty to retreat, retreat could be an important part of the success or failure of a self-defense claim. Whether the defendant retreated could have a profound impact on the reasonableness of their use of deadly force in the situation. Would deadly force have been necessary if they had retreated or would retreat have made no difference? As previously mentioned, wherever possible, the best course of action is always the one that will help you avoid violence and the use of force, deadly or not. Under common law, the defendant claiming self-defense must be able to show or prove that they had retreated before resorting to deadly force in their defense against the attack. The exceptions to this rule are if a safe retreat was not possible or if the attack happened in the defendant's own home. Additionally, under the Model Penal Code, one must either retreat or comply with an attacker if it is completely safe to do so. While the Model Penal Code is not an official law, many courts across the country rely heavily on its principles when dealing with criminal proceedings.

Defense of Others

Okay, so now you know how the use of deadly force relates to self-defense but what about the defense of others, friends, family, even strangers?

The laws governing the defense of others in America closely mirror the laws of personal self-defense. When they believe that someone else is in imminent danger of harm, an individual is permitted to use force in the defense of another and that includes deadly force is absolutely necessary. However, as with many things in life, it's not quite as simple as making a decision to step in when you feel that someone is in danger.

The defense of others is a viable defense against criminal charges but there is much left up to the jury to decide. For instance, it is in the jury's hands to interpret the findings and decide whether the individual was right in their response to the danger or threat.

For the defense of others to apply:
- The individual must have had the belief that the person they are defending was in imminent danger from a threat that would cause them either serious physical injury or even death.
- The individual must have responded reasonably in a way in which any other reasonable person in a similar situation would have responded to the occurrence.
- The individual must have used a reasonable and proportional amount of force against the threat that is not excessive and is

the same kind of force that any other reasonable person would have used in response to a similar situation.

- In both self-defense and defense of others, reasonableness is extremely important. It is not enough for an individual to believe that force is necessary. It must be proven that any reasonable person would have acted in a similar way if they were to face a similar threat.

Furthermore, the response and force used must not only be reasonable. The individual must have used the same force against the threat that the victim would have used in their own self-defense. If the victim wouldn't have used the kind of force against the threat, the individual stepping in to defend them doesn't have a legal leg to stand on and may well end up being charged criminally.

A person stepping in to defend another must carefully assess the situation before jumping to conclusions. It isn't good enough to simply assume that someone is under threat of harm as assumptions can be misleading. A careful judgment about the situation must be made to avoid criminal charges where your assumption could be completely wrong.

For example, a person may stumble upon two people sparring or play-fighting. They may react to what they see by jumping to the conclusion that it is a real fight. In this case, the person may assume the person who seems to have the upper hand is the aggressor and that the person who appears to be losing needs help in their own defense. If this person then steps in and gets involved, the person perceived as being the aggressor may be injured in earnest. The law of defense of others would not stand up against criminal charges as there was no threat to begin with, and the force used in the perceived defense of another was entirely unnecessary.

The following must be met for the law of defense of others to be applicable, but not without limitations:

- There should be some form of relationship between the individual providing defense against the threat and the victim.
- The person who is defending against the threat must not have provoked or initiated the attack or confrontation.
- The person's knowledge of the attacker at the time of the attack will be used to assess the reasonableness of the response and force used. Should it later emerge that the attacker has committed serious violent crimes before but that the individual was unaware of this, the new information will not be taken into account as part of their defense of the victim.
- If the individual and the victim were engaged in criminal activity at the time of the incident, the defense of others will not apply if force is used to overpower an innocent or a potential victim of the criminal activity or to resist arrest.

Deadly Force, Self-Defense and Defense of Others

There is an old adage that says "Don't bring a knife to a gunfight." The reverse is true of self-defense or the defense of others. There are situations in which deadly force is acceptable for both your own self-defense and in the defense of others. However, those situations need careful consideration. It is not acceptable to panic at a perceived threat and to go in 'guns blazing'. In any form of defense of self or others, the force used must not be reasonable and, thus, not excessive. You cannot justify using a firearm against an unarmed attacker. The firearm automatically counts as deadly force whereas the attacker isn't capable of that level of force if they are unarmed.

Many people misconstrue having a firearm for personal safety for 'just in case.' However, as a responsible gun owner, that does not mean that you have the right to wield it without careful consideration and good judgment. You need to assess the situation carefully and determine whether the threat is a real threat or simply perceived, whether the force you are going to use is excessive in the circumstances, and whether your use of that force in that situation is reasonable. A gun is not a simple solution to every possible case of perceived threat. Part of responsible gun ownership is having the knowledge and being able to discern when to use it and when not to.

Chapter 6:

How To Handle Self-Defense

Owning a firearm for personal protection is not something anyone should ever take lightly. Unfortunately, there are far too many gun owners who don't take it nearly seriously enough. A firearm is a very powerful and potentially deadly weapon. Respect for its power is the first step to responsible gun ownership. So, what do you need to know about carrying a firearm for self-defense?

First and foremost, prevention is better than cure. The only fool-proof way to win in a situation of violence is to avoid violent confrontation completely. If you don't get entangled in a struggle or a shootout, you cannot lose.

Secondly; only ever use a firearm in self-defense as a very last resort. Never try to use it to resolve arguments or anything that isn't a life or death situation where an innocent life may be saved.

Important note: This chapter only scrapes the surface of what you need to know about carrying and using a gun for self-defense. It's about filling you in on the bare basics of the matter and is by no means an exhaustive guide.

When Is Shooting Appropriate?

There is no cut and dry answer for when shooting is appropriate for self-defense. To compound the difficulty of answering that question, different jurisdictions have different views on the matter. You shouldn't be asking yourself whether you have the authority or right to defend your own life or that of a loved one or to shoot. The question you should really be asking yourself is whether your local DA or attorney will think that your response was reasonable and justified. They ask themself whether or not they can convince the jury that your actions were not reasonable or justified and that it was unnecessary or the use of excessive force. Juries are made up of individuals of varying beliefs and opinions, especially about the heated topic of firearms, and nothing about the decision-making process is a given.

Don't ask "Can I shoot?" Ask yourself, "Do I really have to shoot?" If the answer isn't "If I don't shoot, this person will kill me or do me serious harm," you probably don't have to resort to shooting.

Elements of Self-Defense

Admissible shooting in self-defense consists of several elements. All of these elements must exist at the same time for an increased chance of DA not pressing criminal charges. However, there is still no guarantee that it won't happen.

The first two elements are:

- You are an innocent victim under attack.
- There is an imminent and legitimate threat to your life or physical safety.

Once those two elements are established, the following needs to be proven:

The ability of your attacker to cause grievous bodily harm or death. Often this means that they are armed. If they are not armed, they must be of substantially greater size, strength, or skill so as to be able to overpower you. Such instances include someone who is considerably larger or stronger than you or who is trained in such as martial arts or boxing. Ask the question: "Does this person have the ability to cause serious bodily harm?"

At the same time as having the ability, your attacker must have the opportunity to cause grievous harm. A firearm is a lethal weapon at close and long-range, presenting an immediate threat, even at a distance. A knife or baseball bat, for instance, is only a real threat at close range. The range at which a threat is effective is an important factor. Ask the questions: "Is the threat immediate?" and "Could I safely retreat, run away, get in my car, and drive away?"

Your attacker must provide intent to imminently cause harm by either verbalization or actions. The intent is often not verbalized as it is mentally processed and your perception of your attacker's actions is what prompts you to respond in self-defense. Are you convinced that you are in imminent danger of harm and will the jury find your attacker's actions to be convincingly indicative of their intention to do so? Intent is very difficult to prove and relies on your reasonable belief that the threat is legitimate enough to respond in self-defense.

You must have absolutely no other option but to shoot in order to save your life. You must be able to convince a jury that there was no other reasonable option except to use deadly force to save your life. When it comes to shooting in self-defense as an affirmative defense in court, saying "I wasn't thinking clearly" isn't going to cut it.

In most instances, you must not have been the one to initiate a confrontation. If you started a physical altercation, didn't back down, and the other person uses extreme force in their own self-defense, shooting them to then defend your own life isn't going to go down well. Avoid being the continued aggressor if the other party backs down. If you didn't start the altercation but the initial aggressor backs down or retreats, you must never continue to use force by going after them as the use of deadly force could have been avoided by simply stopping.

Force on Force Continuum

The Force on Force Continuum is something that is used by security officers and members of law enforcement to decide how much force is acceptable to be used in any situation. It is used to clarify the increase in force a reasonable person is able to apply in any situation and needs to be taken into consideration when responding in self-defense.

In a nutshell, it states that the response to force must be appropriate and start with the least amount of force and increase depending on the attacker's response to your force.

- Verbal orders for the aggressor to back down.
- Physical restraint to prevent the attacker from using force.
- Non-lethal force such as a Taser, pepper spray, etc to stop the attacker.
- Deadly force to stop an imminent threat of serious bodily harm or death—this is only the last resort after all other options have failed.

Only the reasonable and necessary amount of force to stop a threat is permissible. You cannot simply respond to a threat with deadly force or respond to a mild threat with a force that is in excess of what is necessary to prevent harm. Generally speaking, you are allowed to use a similar amount of force as is used by the attacker. If your attacker is advancing on you using verbal force, you cannot respond by shooting them as this is more force than the attacker is using and would be deemed unreasonable and unnecessary. If your attacker doesn't back down and continues to advance, throwing the first punch, you are then entitled to use an equal amount of physical force. Again, simply shooting would be excessive.

However, let's say that your attacker doesn't respond to verbal commands to back down, and continues advancing. He draws a deadly weapon such as a knife when in close proximity to you and verbally expresses the intent to kill. Then, your actions of shooting in self-defense may be justifiable. Your attacker has the ability in the form of an apparent deadly weapon, the opportunity to use it in close proximity, and has stated the intent to do harm or kill. Your shooting in self-defense may be justified but nothing is guaranteed and you need to constantly be asking yourself throughout the experience, "What if?"

"What will happen if I don't shoot my attacker?" and "What will happen if I do shoot this person?"

Difference in Force

Deadly force can only be used in extreme cases in which you are in fear of your life or serious harm. Often this means that a weapon is present but not always. Sometimes there can be a considerable difference in force that creates a grave threat. Being outnumbered or outmatched in skill or strength may also present a very serious threat. However, no hard and fast rule exists as to what constitutes a considerable difference in force.

Competing Harms

The competing harms doctrine is employed in some states and allows an intended victim to use any reasonable and necessary means possible to save their own life, even if that means breaking the law. If there is a reasonable belief that you or another is under imminent threat of harm or death and the necessity and urgency are justifiable, the need to save a life outweighs the criminal offense committed. This includes justifiable homicide.

Justifiable Homicide

There is no self-defense law. There is only self-defense as a defense against criminal charges. Taking a life is taking a life under the law, irrespective of the reason. Thus, all cases where a life is taken start out as a homicide investigation and charge. It is up to the jury or the county, general, or district attorney to discern whether your actions were justifiable under a claim of self-defense and the law. If your actions are justifiable, it will be termed justifiable homicide which means you are guilty of committing homicide but it was a justifiable act in the eyes of the law.

Transferred Intent

The transferred intent doctrine is applied in criminal law when an attacker's intent to harm a person results in the harming of another. According to law, the person causing harm has the intent to cause harm. What does that really mean? If you use deadly force by shooting at an attacker, accidentally missing, and injuring an innocent bystander as collateral damage the intent to harm is transferred from your attacker to the bystander. Regardless of what happened between your attacker and yourself, you face the possibility of being charged with second-degree murder.

Protection of Property

While this is not self-defense, strictly speaking, the question often comes up as to whether a firearm may be used to protect property. There is no clear answer to this one either and again it will depend on the circumstances and the reasonableness of your actions, as well as your ability to persuade the jury. Most of the time it is not justifiable to shoot a perpetrator in the protection of property. The exception is that some states justify it as a preventative measure against arson. Some jurisdictions may allow brandishing a firearm to protect property but this is subject to individual jurisdiction laws as there are those who consider merely brandishing a gun as the use of deadly force.

What if a robbery is taking place in your home? Various states enact the castle doctrine for the protection of your home. However, shooting an unarmed robber equates to unreasonable and unnecessary use of excessive deadly force. If there is no serious threat of grave harm or death to you or anyone else, it will not be deemed a justifiable homicide. Simply breaking and entering does not warrant the use of deadly force or even the use of force greater than verbal commands unless the perpetrator turns violent and poses a greater threat. In the case of an unknown would-be attacker, retreat and calling law enforcement is your safest course of action.

If it comes down to the necessity to shoot an intruder in your home, there are several steps to consider taking. Showing restraint, verifying your target, and employing lesser means of force according to the force continuum first will be your best bet for a favorable defense in court.

When the Threat Stops

When using a firearm in self-defense, the aim is to stop the threat and nothing more. The number of shots that need to be fired for the threat to stop depends on the threat. In an emergency situation, many things happen. You experience an adrenaline rush, you may have tunnel vision, a higher pain threshold, your hearing may be affected, and your fine motor skills may be lessened. All of this happens to the perpetrator as well. Due to these experiences, a single shot may not be enough to stop the threat, the aggressor may not even realize that they have been shot. In this case, an aggressor may not stop attacking until their body stops working due to injuries sustained, such as blood loss. This makes answering the question of "When is enough, enough?" very difficult to answer. The most basic answer is that you shoot to stop the threat, if that takes 10 shots, then that is what it takes. However, once the threat is over, stop shooting. Even if your target is only seriously injured and not killed, you must stop shooting and not continue until they are dead. Once the imminent threat stops, so must you.

Shooting in Self-Defense

Let's say someone used deadly force and threatened you, and possibly your family, in the sanctity of your own home. This could happen anywhere, even on the street. The confrontation has been heated, the risk high, everything seemed to have happened in the blink of an eye, and now there is a lifeless body sprawled out in front of you. You followed all the right steps, as detailed above, about the force-on-force continuum and acting with restraint until there was no other option but having been pushed into taking such a drastic measure is still a very traumatic experience. However, now that all is said and done, what do you do now, and what is going to happen?

The United States holds that it is unconstitutional to take the opinion of guilty until proven innocent. However, when it comes to crime, the law will treat you like a criminal until you are proven either innocent or justified in your actions. When you shoot someone in self-defense, you may feel justified and as though it is a slap in the face but you can expect to be arrested and even charged with a crime. The first day or two after a self-defense shooting is crucial. So, what do you do now?

On average, it takes law enforcement around 11 minutes to respond. While you wait for that response, your decisions and actions are some of the most important you can make so it's imperative to do everything right that you possibly can.

Once the threat has been neutralized, and as long as no threat to your life or safety remains, place your weapon on safety and holster it. A holstered weapon will show law enforcement that you do not pose a threat to them.

Observe the crime scene, it will be treated as a crime scene by police. Make mental notes of important aspects such as the placement of the body and the attacker's weapon. These will be important factors to prove that the attacker was a threat.

Calling 911

Be the first person to call 911 after a self-defense shooting and don't wait too long to do it. Calm yourself before placing the call. It is a subconscious perception that the first person to make the call is the victim. You don't want a bystander or the attacker themselves to be the first to make the call as it doesn't stand you in good stead at all.

911 operators are trained to keep callers on the line to gather as much information as possible. This is done to help first responders deal with the situation as quickly and effectively as possible. However, your mental and emotional state is not taken into account. There is a very real risk that if you are prompted with questions, you're going to say something potentially incriminating. That's not to say that you mean to say something that may be misconstrued as an admission of guilt. You don't want a long and rambling voice recording, to get flustered by questions, and to give a prosecutor any advantage. A prosecutor's job is to prove that you are guilty of a crime, even if you're an innocent victim. That's just how the system works. However, even your demeanor and tone of voice could be used. In addition, each word you say and how you phrase things will be dissected. Your words and actions following a self-defense shooting will impact your case greatly.

Be mindful of the fact that 911 calls are recorded and archived to be used as evidence. They are also still recording while you are put on hold. Be aware that anything you say or do while on hold is being recorded and can also be used against you in a criminal case.

When speaking with 911, they have no authority over you. You are not obligated to answer any of the questions they ask you, nor are you required to comply with anything they tell you to do or not to do. This gives you some power over how much information you divulge and what you tell them.

Your call to 911 has only one purpose—to bring help to the scene. You are reporting the incident and there is no other objective for the call. Do not try to give them a reason for the shooting, make a statement, express emotion, plead your case, or try to get assurance that you weren't in the wrong by shooting an attacker. The more time you spend talking, the greater the risk that you will say something that you either shouldn't or don't mean.

Here's what you should be telling the operator:

- Don't use incriminating words such as "killed." If possible mention nothing about shooting the attacker at all.

- Your full name.
- The street address you are calling from.
- Tell them that you have been a victim of a crime.
- Request the necessary responding services, such as an ambulance and police.
- Tell them where you are at the address (in the master bedroom, for instance).
- Provide a description of yourself so that responders know who you are and what you look like.

Once you have provided all the absolutely essential information to the 911 dispatcher, simply hang up. Don't ask whether you can hang up, just hang up. The next call you want to make should be to your lawyer. The sooner, the better.

Excited Utterances

An excited utterance is something said in the wake of a shocking experience. You respond spontaneously to an event, such as a self-defense shooting, by blurting out thoughts and emotions. Your natural fight or flight instinct would have kicked in during the ordeal and bombarded your body with adrenaline and hormones. This has a profound effect on your body and mind. Some negative side effects include hearing problems, tunnel vision, distortion of time, and even emotional detachment or feeling completely numb. The effects can be felt up to hours afterward and some physical reactions to this massive dose of adrenaline may include exhaustion, vomiting, and the urge to pace, fidget, or talk non-stop. Your mind and body won't be doing you any favors and you may have trouble remembering details of what happened and describing the situation correctly. You may say or do things out of the ordinary or that you don't really mean to.

Unfortunately, during this time of adrenaline-fueled confusion, you will have to deal with the police. During this time, they will observe and take note of everything that you do or say and your actions and words can quite easily set the investigation's tone. Being careful about excited utterances is of the utmost importance as you might mean to say one thing but how you say it could be misinterpreted by another to be an admission of guilt or wrongdoing.

Witnesses and Bystanders

If you were not alone during the incident and there are bystanders or witnesses to the shooting, don't discuss anything with them. If someone poses the question whether you are alright, the only answer you should provide them with is that you might be in shock. Again, if you engage in conversation or elaborate on how you are feeling, you could say something that could be used against you later.

The Crime Scene

Under absolutely no circumstances should you touch anything at the crime scene. You are not obligated to provide your attacker with medical assistance and, if you don't have medical training, you shouldn't be trying. As nonsensical as it may seem, trying to help your attacker could actually land you in hot water for tampering with evidence. Try to distance yourself from the scene but not too far away. While waiting for responders to arrive, create a mental grid of the scene and where each person and item of possible evidence is within that grid. Investigators will go through the scene with a fine-toothed comb and take statements from any possible witnesses.

Making a mental note of the scene and even of where witnesses were standing helps to safeguard you from other's possible mistakes. Someone standing 30 or 40 feet away may state that they heard absolutely every single word clearly when in fact they were too far away to have heard anything but shouting. In this case, you want to be able to question their testimony. Remember that witnesses may be just as much in shock as you are and may not be able to recall things accurately.

If you are injured in the altercation, don't clean up or address your injuries unless they are very serious and need immediate temporary attention before an ambulance arrives. This will allow your injuries sustained in the confrontation to be documented as evidence.

Questioning

Once the police have secured the area and made sure that there is no further threat, you included, the questions will start flying. It is important to cooperate with law enforcement but do so respectfully and as minimally as possible. Don't consent to a search, even if one will be performed anyway. Answer basic questions, if necessary; otherwise, exercise your right to remain silent until you have spoken with an attorney. It's usually a good idea to tell the police that you don't want to answer any questions until you have spoken with an attorney. Do not just give them the silent treatment. Tell any family members who may be present not to answer any questions until they have also spoken with an attorney.

Far from making a statement, provide law enforcement with key case facts, such as identifying the attacker and their weapon. Resist divulging too much information but key elements should be identified. Just as what you do say could be used against you; there are some things that could work against you if you don't say them. Stick to the basics.

You might be arrested; be mentally and emotionally prepared to be taken into police custody. Continue to exercise your right to remain silent, even with potential cellmates. They may be called as witnesses and provide testimony about what you did and said while in custody.

Some individuals might think it a good idea to provide responders with a pre-printed card with a basic, generic statement instead of trying to memorize their rights. Some may also think it's a good idea to mention that they have a legal service plan in case of shooting in self-defense. This is a bad idea as the prosecution may point to this action to prove that the incident was premeditated.

Try to be alone when you contact your attorney. Anyone who may be close enough to overhear your conversation may misconstrue what you are saying or act as a witness in court.

If you are in any way injured in the altercation or suspect that you may have been injured, inform the police and request to be taken to a hospital for evaluation. Adrenaline overloads the body with chemicals that could mask the sensations of pain and you may not even realize that you are injured. Other times, injuries may not be blatantly visible. For instance, if, before the shooting, part of the confrontation was physical, you may have sustained internal injuries in the process.

Write Everything Down

As soon as you possibly can, write everything that you can remember about the incident down. It can help to jot down the details while they are still fresh in your mind in preparation for meeting with your attorney and making your statement.

What you should write down:

- What was said by you and your attacker? (Try to remember exactly the words used.)
- What actions by your attacker caused you to respond with a deadly weapon and shoot?
- How long did the confrontation between you and your attacker last?
- Were there any witnesses and, if so, how many?
- Where were you coming from at the time of the incident?
- Where were you going when the incident happened?
- What were you wearing at the time of the incident?
- When were weapons drawn during the confrontation?

The Morning After

Killings, even in self-defense, make the news so you need to be prepared for the media attention. Should you be permitted to go home, you may well find news crews, photographers, and other curious people trying to find out what happened. Any invasion of private property should be reported to the police. If the media are on the sidewalk or in the street, let them be and try your best to ignore them.

Never speak to anybody in the media and never allow family members or close friends to speak to them either. It doesn't matter how they try to provoke a reaction or an answer from you, don't give in. Anything you say and do that is captured by the media will be admitted as evidence at trial. Try to stay out of sight, draw the curtains if you have to, and avoid leaving your home unless necessary. Prepared to be holed up at home for a week or two until things cool down and the media attention is drawn by another incident.

If police obtain a search warrant for your home, regardless of where the incident took place, ensure that all firearms are correctly and safely stored before they arrive. Firearms lying around, even if they are completely unloaded, doesn't look good or responsible.

10 Mistakes to Avoid

Don't do anything while in panic mode. A panicked mind is misleading and can make you say or do things that may incriminate you or make you look guilty of a crime. Resist the urge to say or do anything until you have calmed down.

Don't leave the scene. With the exception of being in danger, resist the urge to leave the scene or seek out the comfort of friends or family. Stay at the scene, even if everything seems too overwhelming to handle. Leaving may be misconstrued as fleeing the scene which gives the impression of guilt.

Never touch the crime scene. Trying to move or touch anything unnecessarily will lead authorities to assume that you are trying to hide something, tamper with evidence, or interfere with the investigation to follow. Make sure to tell any witnesses or bystanders not to touch anything within the scene.

Don't be surprised when you are treated like a criminal. Prepare yourself for being treated like you are guilty of wrongdoing. It is the police's job to treat you as a possible suspect until they know what has happened and established the facts. If they don't handle you as a possible suspect, they are leaving themselves open to letting a criminal go. After all, criminals will say and do whatever they must to seem innocent and get out of the situation. Cooperate with police, allow them to arrest you without resistance, if they arrest you, and just let things happen as they do without protest.

Don't make a statement to anyone before consulting your attorney. This cannot be reiterated enough. When you shoot someone, even in self-defense, silence is golden. The 5th Amendment is there for a reason, so make use of it. Doing otherwise could lead you to say or admitting things you don't mean when you aren't thinking clearly.

Don't be fooled by the good cop/bad cop technique. When you have been through a traumatic event, you will likely want to talk to a sympathetic ear. It's natural to want to "let it all out" and state your version of events. Don't fall for it.

Don't have your gun in your hand when law enforcement or first responders arrive. If you shoot someone in self-defense, chances are someone will have called 911 to report shots fired. If this is the case, the police won't know who the victim is and who the attacker is. If you have a gun in your hand when they arrive, they will view you as a threat and treat you like one. Holster your gun or set it down with the safety on so that you don't appear as a potential threat.

Don't lecture the police about anything and don't get angry. Law enforcement officers are only human and will respond to lectures and belligerence like any other human being. Don't belittle them, don't talk down to them, don't challenge their authority. Even if you believe something they do or say is not accurate or right, don't get into a debate about it; you are only going to get their backs up and make your life more difficult during the investigation.

Don't forget courtesy and respect for law enforcement. Law enforcement has been getting a bad rap in recent times but you shouldn't automatically assume that all law enforcement officers are bad apples. Treat them with respect and courtesy; "sir" and "ma'am" go a long way to showing respect and getting on their good side.

Don't give in to trying your case at the scene or at any time until you have consulted with your lawyer. Police don't just use the good cop/bad cop routine to get a reaction from investigation suspects. They may try to challenge your use of a deadly weapon in the altercation. You may want to argue because you're the victim and being treated like a criminal may be infuriating and frustrating. Nothing you can say to the police will let you off the hook without an investigation so don't give in to the urge.

Chapter 7:

Responsible Gun Ownership

Firearms are deadly weapons that must be treated with a healthy amount of respect and more than just a dash of responsibility. This is to ensure your own safety and the safety of others. Even if your gunmanship is on point, you still need to maintain a responsible attitude toward that weapon. Any lapse in responsibility could lead to injury or even a fatality. Let's take a closer look at principles responsible gun ownership.

Rules and Mindset

Gun safety is an attitude and mindset instilled and maintained by consistently following certain safety rules when you own a firearm. Mark Handbury Beaufoy, an English game shooting lover and politician, wrote some verses on gun safety that are regularly quoted. These verses include various notable points. The "A Father's Advice" verses he wrote begins with:

If a sportsman true you'd be

Listen carefully to me:

Never, never, let your gun

Pointed be at anyone...

Another source of notable gun safety advice is The A B C of Rifle, 1913, by Ira L. Reeves in which he states the following:

"The Accident-Proof Rule": "The muzzle of a firearm should never point in a direction in which, if discharged, it would do injury where an injury is not meant to be done."

"the companion rule of the one just given": "All firearms are at all times loaded."

And he went on to say: "The trigger should never be pulled until the identity of the thing fired at has been established beyond any doubt." (Wikipedia, 2020)

When it comes to gun safety, there is a list of 10 commandments or principles that must be followed to promote responsible gun ownership.

- Treat every firearm respectfully as if it's loaded.
- Only bring empty guns, with the action open or taken down, into a home, vehicle, or camp.
- Ensure that the barrel and action are always obstruction-free.
- Always carry a gun in such a way that you are in control of the muzzle direction.
- Be positive about your intended target before pulling the trigger.
- Do not point a firearm at something you don't intend to shoot, ever.
- Unless unloaded, never leave a gun unattended.
- Don't ever climb obstacles, such as a fence or tree, with a loaded firearm.
- Never shoot at the water's surface or a surface that is flat and hard.
- Never drink and handle a firearm.

The United States Marine Corps employs the following four safe gun handling rules:

- Handle every firearm as if it's loaded.
- Do not ever point a firearm at something you don't want to shoot.
- Keep your trigger finger, your index finger) straight and off the trigger until you are ready to fire your weapon.
- Keep your gun safety on until you are ready to shoot.

Important note: Even blank ammunition is dangerous, up to 15 feet in fact. Individuals have been killed or injured because of the belief that blanks aren't dangerous. The same firearm safety rules apply to blanks as life ammunition.

Now that you have a rundown of some general gun safety principles, let's take a closer look at the most critical to provide a better understanding of why they are important to follow.

Treat Every Firearm Respectfully as if It's Loaded

The point of this rule is to maintain vigilance in the presence of guns. Treating a firearm as if it is loaded will cultivate safe firearm handling habits. It will also prevent you from falling into the trap of presuming that unsafe practices are acceptable because "I know my firearm is unloaded so it's okay." Maintaining the attitude that a gun is always loaded, even when you know it's not, will stop you from relying on that presumption until it is proven that the firearm is unloaded. This goes a long way to avoiding unintentional discharge. Always treating a gun as loaded by following safe practices will also help prevent injury, damage, or death in the case of an accidental discharge.

Many gun-related accidents happen as a result of an individual mistaking it as safetied, empty, or disarmed in any way and it turns out that the gun is actually ready to fire. These misunderstandings can happen for a variety of reasons.

- Faulty gun handling where an individual incorrectly executes loading, firing, and emptying, does it in the wrong order, or skips steps in the process.

- Mistaken beliefs about the status of the gun. This could be the belief that the safety is on when it isn't or believing the chamber or magazine is empty when there is still one or more rounds in either. It may also arise from an incorrect presumption that the firearm is in a particular state and not checking whether that assumption is true. An example may be passing a gun between two people. Assuming that the first person has checked the status of the firearm and the second person not double-checking it could result in injury. Never assume anything about a weapon except that it may be loaded.

- Mechanical failures due to faulty parts or assembly, wear and tear, damage to the weapon, or even a faulty design may lead to accidents. Be vigilant about the condition of your firearm. A worn safety may cause it not to work even when it appears to be on. Worn or damaged parts in the sear, hammer, or trigger could cause an overly sensitive trigger, otherwise known as a hair-trigger. A fault in the shape of the body of the gun could cause it to jam or discharge prematurely. Impact sensitivity causes a discharge unintentionally when the gun strikes an object. A faulty extractor could leave a round in the chamber even if you have taken the correct steps to unload the firearm.

Treating a firearm as if it has the capability to discharge at any moment makes you more likely to employ practices that will avoid unintentional discharge.

Always Point the Muzzle Away From Unintended Targets

This rule is also known as muzzle discipline and the point of it is to avoid potential injury, damage, or death due to an unintentional discharge. The first step in the process is to follow the rule of treating a firearm as loaded. The second step in the process is to never point it at something you don't intend to shoot. If you treat it as loaded, you can assume that it could discharge, and ensuring that the muzzle is pointed away from anything you don't intend to shoot avoids unnecessary accents if it does fire.

Following this rule will ensure that you don't entertain any playing around with a gun as aiming playfully at non-targets is in violation of the rule. When handling a firearm, there are two generally safe directions in which to point a firearm; the sky and the ground. However, neither is foolproof. Shooting at the ground could cause a ricochet or dangerous fragments to be propelled at non-targets. Pointing your gun skyward carries the risk of the bullet causing damage or harm to a non-target when it makes its way back to earth. As they say, what goes up must come down.

Important Note: Firing a gun straight into the air results in the bullet coming back down at much less speed than it went up. If the gun is fired at an angle into the air, it maintains its spin and thus it's ballistic stability. This means it won't tumble through the air as a round shot straight up may do on its way back down. Firing upward but at an angle allows the bullet to reach and maintain much deadlier speeds.

Indoor handling of a firearm may negate the possibility of pointing the muzzle upward or downward, especially in multistory buildings. If you are going to regularly be handling a gun indoors, investigate and designate a safe direction to always point the muzzle. An idea is to create a 'cleaning barrel' by filling a container with sand. This will stop the bullet and prevent ricochets in the case of an unintentional discharge.

Finger Straight and off the Trigger

This rule is also known as trigger discipline. The point of this rule is to avoid unintentional discharge. When your finger is on the trigger, you may experience an involuntary movement of that finger which may result in pulling the trigger and firing the weapon. This may happen because you are given a fright, you may not be paying attention to your body movements, you may stumble or fall, you may experience an involuntary spasm or twitch. You may also unintentionally cause your finger to be squeezed against the trigger, as may be the case of trying to holster a weapon with the safety off and your finger still on the trigger. Always keep your trigger finger, usually your index finger, straight and off the trigger until such time as you are ready to fire.

Be Positive of Your Target and What's Around it

The point of this rule is to make sure that you know exactly what you are shooting and that you are aware of any potential collateral damage. Non-targets around or behind the target should be taken into account if something were to go wrong during the shooting. Positively identifying a target and verifying that identity will prevent you from shooting a non-target. Identifying what is around and behind your target will prevent collateral damage if the bullet misses the target and hits something else.

There are three reasons why identifying all non-targets around your intended target is important:

- The bullet may miss the target and hit a non-target behind it.
- A non-target may move in between you and your target and be hit by the bullet.
- The shot may be a through-and-through, passing through the target and hitting a non-target behind it.

Mechanical Malfunctions

Firearm mechanical malfunctions include things like jamming, the breech or barrel failing to contain the round, accidental firing pin release, out-of-battery discharges, and slam fires.

Jamming

Jamming includes failure to feed, extract, or eject the cartridge, failure to lock back when empty for gas-operated and recoil firearms, and failure to cycle completely after discharge. A failure to lock back when empty is mainly a procedural danger. The "slide lock" offers the shooter a visual indication that the supply of ammunition is finished.

When a firearm jams it should be treated with extreme care. When the primer of a cartridge has been struck and it has been deformed due to a jam it could discharge out of the blue and without warning. This is known as a hang fire.

Out-of-Battery Discharge

Out-of-battery discharges happen when the bolt does not properly secure the cartridge but the round can be discharged by the firing pin. These discharges could be triggered as a slam fire or by purposefully releasing the firing pin. Out-of-battery discharges regularly cause a great deal of damage to the firearm itself; to the magazine, firing pin, and the receiver in particular. Common injuries to the handler include damage to the eyes and even being blinded. Using shooting glasses is recommended to avoid the potential of eye injury due to an out-of-battery discharge. Avoiding the malfunction is possible through building an understanding of the gun's operating mechanism.

Slam Firing

Slam firing happens then the cartridge discharges immediately when it is chambered but before the trigger is squeezed. Slam fires more commonly happen in firearms with a floating firing pin, the firing pin moves freely within the receiver or bolt and becomes clogged with debris or when a cartridge case primer is not properly raised. Slam firing may also be the result of a softer than normally recommended cartridge primer being used.

There are also several other reasons a firearm may experience an unintentional misfire, including receiving hard mechanical shocks and being dropped. It may also happen if the trigger is faulty or when the round is cooked off due to the build-up of excessive heat in the chamber. You can prevent unintentional discharges by using a modern gun design that has up-to-date safety features such as a firing pin block. This prevents the primer being struck by the firing pin except when the trigger is pulled. If you have an older gun that does not have more modern safety features, you should carry the firearm without a round in the chamber or, if you have a revolver, the firing pin should be resting on an empty chamber.

Catastrophic Failure

A very serious malfunction that firearms may experience is called a catastrophic failure or a kaBoom (kB). These are failures from which the firearm cannot be recovered and may cause grievous injuries to the handler. For instance, if the barrel is blocked by foreign material, the round has nowhere to go and cannot be expelled by the weapon. In this instance, the round may explode backward, causing the barrel to blow up or the firearm to explore toward the handler. There are various causes, such as mishandling the firearm, weakened or damaged parts, and bad firearm design. Another reason for a catastrophic failure is when a handler uses ammunition the firearm wasn't designed to use but can still be chambered and fired by the weapon.

As explained in the example above, catastrophic failure may also be caused by a blockage in the barrel caused by debris such as dirt or even snow or water. To avoid such blockages, never let the muzzle of your firearm rest on the ground or moisture, such as rain, accumulate in the barrel.

Mishandling can cause serious problems and increase the risk of malfunction. Using a cartridge that creates more pressure than the gun was designed to handle. Reasons for this include using overpressure ammunition, using magnum loads in weapons not rated for those loads, or improper handloading.

Failure to Fire

Various malfunctions are linked to the gun's firing pin or the primer and/or powder within a specific round. These include hang fire or delayed firing, misfires or a failure to fire, and squibs or discharge in which the round does not receive enough force to leave the barrel and could, as a result, get stuck.

When a gun misfires, the round doesn't discharge after the firing pin strikes it. In a hang fire, the round is struck by the firing pin but firing is delayed by a few seconds. For a squib malfunction, there may not be sufficient powder inside the round, causing it to get stuck in the bore. If a handler tries to fire a second round while an unfired round is stuck in the bore or barrel, the barrel could peel back, causing severe damage to both the weapon and the handler.

In any case of a failure to fire, the handler of the firearm should wait between 25 seconds and two minutes before cautiously removing the magazine and removing any misfired or misfed rounds. The gun should be pointed in a safe direction where it poses no threat to non-targets and the breech should be carefully opened to check that there are no blockages of the barrel or bore. If there are any misfed rounds, they should be properly disposed of and not just thrown into the trash. A common way to dispose of misfed rounds is to use a special container designed for live ammunition that has failed to fire.

Storage

Proper firearm storage is important, irrespective of what kind of gun you have. Proper storage prevents not only the theft of guns and ammunition or firearms being used without permission but also prevents them from getting damaged. A damaged firearm is a dangerous firearm, as has been explained under the section of malfunctions.

There are several storage options to suit your particular needs as a gun owner.

Gun Safes

Gun safes prevent physical access to the firearm and local laws may dictate specific standards when it comes to strength, theft resistance, locks. Your state may also require you to store weapons and ammunition separately.

Disassembling

Disassembling your firearm and storing the parts in separate places prevents others from accessing a functioning weapon. The law of your state may even stipulate this rule for storing firearms. So it's always a good idea to check the laws applicable to your state.

Trigger Locks

Trigger locks prevent manipulation of the trigger but aren't foolproof and the firearm may still be capable of being discharged. This type of lock is subject to controversy with regard to manufacturing standards, how they are used, and what the legislature says about them. Trigger locks have been demonstrated to be relatively easy for children to remove with common household items and many weapons may discharge if dropped. Trigger locks also make the time it takes to respond to an emergency self-defense situation longer. If you are thinking about using a trigger lock, check your state laws regarding approved manufacturers.

Chamber Locks

Chamber locks block the chamber with a plug or dummy round to prevent live ammunition from being chambered. Essentially, this type of lock jams the gun to prevent it from being used. Another form of chamber lock uses a key to lock a rod into the safety cartridge which stops the dummy round from being ejected and live ammunition from being loaded.

Cable Locks

Cable locks are pretty popular and commonly work on repeating firearms by threading into the receiver by way of the ejection port. They physically block the bold movement, preventing the gun from cycling and stopping the return to "battery" and the breech from closing. Cable locks may also be threaded through the magazine which prevents it from being properly inserted.

Smart Guns

Smart guns have built-in locks that work with radio frequency identification (RFID) chips to prevent unauthorized use. These guns have a built-in receiver chip that can read a corresponding chip in items such as rings, use fingerprint recognition, magnetism, or even a microchip implanted in the owner.

Separate Ammunition Storage

Ammunition storage stores bullets away from guns in a safe location. This prevents unauthorized use of the firearm because there is no live ammunition in the gun and it cannot be easily accessed. Always store ammunition in a cool, dry place that is not subject to vapors that could contaminate it to prevent the ammunition from deteriorating. If you use a handloading gun, be extra careful with the storage of loose gunpowder and primers.

Gun Safety Around Children

Children account for the most unfortunate and tragic accidental injuries and fatalities related to firearms. Any under-aged children who are not of legal age to own or handle a firearm should be taught a specific set of rules to help them be aware of how to handle a situation where they happen upon a firearm:

- Stop. (Stop whatever you're doing and don't proceed toward the gun.)
- Don't touch. (Leave the gun alone and don't touch it.)
- Leave the area. (Don't play in the area after finding a gun.)
- Tell an adult. (Immediately tell an adult about finding a gun.)

Teaching children these rules aims to prevent them from handling firearms and form part of the Eddie Eagle Program, created by the National Rifle Association.

Whether the parents own a gun or not, it is important to instill these rules in children to prevent injury or death as a result of them finding their parents' guns or those of someone else. However, children are curious and may find it difficult to adhere to these rules, especially when very young. In this case, parents who own guns must ensure that the weapons are always unloaded and that they are securely stored in a safe place and that ammunition is stored separately. Parents should also ensure that their children are safe in the homes of family and friends by asking whether there are any weapons in the house. Make sure that friends and family who do own guns have them stored safely and securely.

Unsafe Handlers

Never use, or even handle, a firearm when under the influence of any form of drugs or alcohol. This may include certain medications that could impair judgment. There are various states that have laws in place in which it is a crime to carry a firearm while under the influence and the penalties are similar to those of driving while under the influence.

Whenever your judgment is impaired in any way, it is not a good idea to even handle a gun, let alone use it. Such instances include dehydration, exhaustion, and stress-related to your emotional state. When you are impaired in any way, your judgment about the intended target or firearm state, cognitive ability, sensory perception, and reaction time is negatively affected.

There are many jurisdictions that forbid the possession and use of firearms by those deemed to be incapable of safely using them, including mentally ill individuals and convicted felons.

Secondary Hazards

When you think of the dangers that come with a firearm, you probably only really think about its primary function; the discharge of ammunition. While this is one of the most hazardous risks of a gun, it isn't the only one. There are various other hazards to the handler and those around them.

Noise

The noise a firearm makes when it is discharged is loud enough to cause either temporary or permanent damage to hearing. Such damage includes loss of hearing and tinnitus or a ringing in the ears. When using a gun outside of emergency self-defense situations, wearing protective gear such as earmuffs, earplugs, or even both will help protect your ears from damage. You may also choose to use a silencer on your firearm, however, it is advisable to check local and state laws regarding silencers in your area.

Hot Gases

Hot gases are emitted from a gun during discharge, as well as powder and other forms of debris. Additionally; various weapons, such as semi and fully automatic firearms usually rapidly eject spent shell casings which are extremely hot at the time of ejection. Any form of gas or debris emitted from a firearm during handling may cause harm to an individual, either the handler or a bystander closely. Various protective gear, such as protective eyewear, should be worn to minimize the risk of injury.

Pollutants and Toxins

Firearms and ammunition are a possible source of pollutants and toxins which could prove hazardous to the health of both the handler and others.

- Acid rain could mobilize lead ammunition discarded in natural areas.
- Older ammunition might have potentially toxic mercury-based primers.
- Shooting range backstops allow the lead to accumulate.
- Other pollutants include powder, lead dust, and smoke emitted into the air through firearm use.
- Copper, lead, and various other materials are released during firearm cleaning, and strong cleaning agents also let off potentially hazardous vapors.

Firearm Use: Training and Practice

The debate about gun control is ongoing, it's been raging for years and it will continue to rage on in the future. Many arguments advocate stricter gun control regulations, which does make sense. After all, the stricter the regulations, the safer the nation, right? To a certain degree that is true. Stricter regulations surrounding gun ownership makes it harder for individuals who may not be suited for gun ownership. However, the one thing that many of these debates seem to overlook is training firearm owners. Different states have different laws regarding firearm training so it is important to check the local and state laws in your area. Some states require training as part of the licensing procedure while others aren't as strict. Regardless of whether your area requires training, it is a vital part of responsible gun ownership.

The unfortunate truth is that many gun owners will walk into a store, buy a firearm, spend only a little time on learning how to handle and shoot the gun, and then not train or practice again. Bear in mind that a firearm is only as good as the handler and the handler is only as good at their training. It's easy enough to understand that shooting at a live target in a real emergency self-defense situation isn't quite the same as firing at an inanimate target at a range. It's not as easy to imagine yourself in that emergency situation where firearm proficiency could be the difference between life or death. Many people cling to the belief that it won't happen to them; therefore, simply owning a gun is enough to put them at ease and they are happy enough to neglect their training and practice. This is one of the biggest mistakes that you, as a gun owner, can make.

Firearm proficiency isn't acquired by attending a one-off training course and then that's it, you're trained. It is an ongoing process that requires regular practice. Any gun owner should make training and practice a priority. Here's why.

This is especially true for new gun owners. It's not enough to purchase a firearm, take a few shots, and Bob's your uncle, you are educated about your firearm. Attending a training course will teach you about responsible gun ownership, good habits, the operation of your gun, the different parts and functions, and how to clean your weapon. All of these things are incredibly important for first-time gun owners and can prevent accidents.

Forgetting Skills

There is the saying "It's like riding a bike; you never forget how to do it." This may be true. If you rode a bike as a kid, chances are you can ride one as an adult even if you haven't been on a bicycle in years. However, all of those stunts you did as a kid aren't going to come naturally to you anymore. You would need to relearn them. It is the same with owning and using a firearm. You may understand and remember the principles of gun safety and use but your aim and reactions are going to be rusty if you haven't had practice since you first bought your gun.

Honing Skills

Part of your obligation and responsibility as a gun owner is to hone your skills as a marksman. It's not good enough to simply know how to safely use a firearm; you need to become skilled at it. An unskilled shooter may miss their intended target, accidentally shoot a non-target due to mishandling, or panic in an emergency situation, and shoot an innocent person mistaken as a threat.

Form and Maintain Good Gun Safety Habits

When you are regularly going to a gun range, the rules of gun safety are constantly refreshed and sound practices are instilled and maintained. When attending a gun range, the range will insist on following the rules of gun safety. When you stop practicing, it is easier to become slack and allow bad gun handling and safety habits to creep in.

Expert Help

Whether you consult a trainer at a range for advice on improving your skills or attend a refresher training course, getting expert help is never a bad idea. A skilled and experienced handler can help you improve your form and skill or help overcome problems you may be experiencing which could hinder you from becoming fully proficient.

Learning New Things

It's easy enough to fall victim to the belief that you already know everything you need to know about owning and handling a firearm. However, this is rarely ever the case. Going to a gun range, practicing, mingling with other gun owners, and having experts around is one of the best ways to open yourself up to the possibility of learning something new. It might even be something as simple as discovering a change in the law that you weren't aware of.

Avoid Failures and Unnecessary Accidents

Many gun-related accidents occur due to faulty parts and a lack of cleaning. When you attend a gun range, handle your weapon, and practice regularly; you gain an intimate knowledge of your weapon and maintain a cleaning schedule. As parts of your gun become worn or faulty over time, you will pick up on those faults quickly and be able to see to them. You will also need to clean your firearm regularly.

Maintenance and cleaning will keep your gun in tip-top shape at all times, avoiding unnecessary accidents or failures in an emergency situation.

Chapter: 8

Marksmanship

Handling firearms starts with the principles of responsible gun ownership and gun safety detailed in the previous chapter on Responsible Gun Ownership. If you've not yet read that chapter and skipped to this one to find out some cool technical information, it's best you go back and read the previous chapter first. Everything starts with safety otherwise the cool things could end up being not so cool when a grievous accident occurs, or worse. Once you're up to speed with the principles and practices of gun safety, we'll move on to marksmanship.

Defining Marksmanship

The definition of a marksman is someone who is trained and skilled in shooting with precision using a projectile weapon, otherwise commonly called firearms. In this day and age, a marksman usually makes use of a firearm with a scope to increase precision. The targets of marksmen are usually high-value shots from a range that is further than average. Typically, marksmen for part of armed forces, such as the military. Marksmanship, therefore, refers to someone's skill and ability shooting a firearm, be it a handgun, such as a pistol, or a long gun, such as a rifle.

A popularized term for a marksman is a sharpshooter and many people use the words interchangeably. However, this is not entirely correct. Within the military and shooting sports, marksman and sharpshooter are terms that markedly different shooting skill levels and are never used synonymously. A specific example is the usage of the words in the United States Army. Here, a marksman is someone who is of a lesser skill level than a sharpshooter. In turn, a sharpshooter is a lower level of skill than an expert. There are four skill levels that are typically recognized today in both United States military and civilian shooting capacities.

- Unqualified.
- Marksman.
- Sharpshooter.
- Expert.

The three upper or qualified shooting skill levels are often awarded marksmanship badges, whether you are part of the military or a civilian shooter.

What about marksmen and snipers? In the military, there is a distinct difference between a marksman and a sniper. A marksman is a qualified shooter who forms a normal part of the military fire team responsible for 'fire and movement' and 'bounding overwatch' in combat. A marksman is never expected to act on their own away from the military's main force. Military marksmen may join an infantry fire team as specifically designated marksmen to support the team through long-range fire at vulnerable targets. In this way, they extend the tactical power of the fire team.

A sniper, however, is part of special ops and often works alone or as part of a small team away from the main force. Their focus is on independent mission goals. The job of a sniper usually involves long-range fire but also doing mission reconnaissance, assessment of combat damage, and coordinates/corrections spotting for artillery fire and airstrikes.

So, where does that leave you, as a civilian gun owner and user? Marksmanship in the United States is a long-standing tradition. The early beginnings of this marksmanship tradition stem from the roles played by ordinary men in the Revolutionary War. Today, there are various organizations that encourage marksmanship in civilian circles. One such organization is the Civilian Marksmanship Program which has its beginnings just shortly after the turn of the 20th century.

The Civilian Marksmanship Program

Otherwise known as CMP, the Civilian Marksmanship Program is a government-chartered program that encourages and provides all qualified United States citizens with proper gun safety training and rifle practice. This program places particular emphasis on firearm safety and practice education for the youth of the nation to promote good firearm handling and care habits and responsible ownership. The idea is to start them young and build a lifetime of good habits and practices to ensure a safer country for all.

It is not compulsory or mandatory to participate in the program. However, providing that they are a member of a club affiliated with CMP, any United States citizen who is not legally barred from owning a gun may purchase a military surplus rifle from CMP.

Being government-chartered, the CMP operates with permission from the United States government but is not a government organization itself. Instead, it operates through a network of privately affiliated organizations, shooting clubs, and state associations, covering each and every state across the United States. Through this extensive network, civilians are offered not only gun safety training and courses in marksmanship but also a chance to pit their skills against others in competitions.

Civilian Marksmanship Program: History

As part of the War Department Appropriations Act of 1903, the United States Congress created the Office of the Director of Civilian Marksmanship or the DMC. Originally, the purpose of creating this office was to offer ordinary qualified civilians the chance to learn and practice marksmanship skills. These skills would then be valuable if they were to be called upon to serve in the United States military at a later date. The formation of the office was necessitated by adopting the M1903 Springfield rifle as the national service firearm. The M1903 rifle had a bold action that was unfamiliar to civilians who were experienced in lever-action rifles that were popular at the time. This put civilians at a disadvantage, if they were to be called upon to serve, as they were not able to maintain a rate of fire with the new rifle that was equivalent to the rate of fire of the popular rifles they were familiar with. So, in essence, the CMP was first created to help train civilians in the newly adopted national service rifle so that they would be able to operate it if they were called to serve their country in a time of need.

As time went on, the focus of the program moved away from training civilians to use the national service rifle and shifted to focus on developing the youth through marksmanship. Between 1916 and 1996 the Civilian Marksmanship Program was run by the United States Army. In 1996 the Corporation for the Promotion of Rifle Practice & Firearms Safety (CPRPFS) was created by Title XVI of the National Defense Authorization Act for the Fiscal Year 1996 (Public Law 104-106, 10 February 1996) to take over running the CMP. The Corporation for the Promotion of Rifle Practice & Firearms Safety is a non-profit, tax-exempt, corporation approved by the United States government but is not an agency of the government. The CMP receives no federal funding aside from surplus .22 and .30 caliber rifles being donated from the United States Army's inventory. The program is entirely civilian funded.

CMP: Facilities, Sales, Programs, Competition

There are three main offices of the CMP:

- CMP South in Anniston, Alabama.
- CMP Talladega Marksmanship Park in Talladega, Alabama.
- CMP North at Camp Perry near Port Clinton, Ohio.

Sales

The sale of surplus United States army rifles is particularly popular and the CMP offers the following for sale:

- M1 Garand.
- M1903 Springfield.
- M1917 Enfield.
- M1 Carbine.
- .22 calibers (surplus and commercial target).
- Air rifles (commercial target).
- M1911 pistol (added in 2018).

All surplus military firearms are only available for sale to members of Civilian Marksmanship Program affiliated clubs, organizations, and associations. The CMP online store also offers ammunition and other accessories for sale.

Programs

The Civilian Marksmanship Program facilitates training that is centered on teaching individuals gun safety, leadership, responsibility, and competitive distinction within shooting sports across the country. It is responsible for sponsoring, supporting, and hosting a variety of competitive pistol and rifle shooting events such as the National Matches at Camp Perry and various national junior air rifle championships. Camps and clinics are held at various locations throughout the year, the most notable of which is the summer camp program which provides camps for three-position air rifle, standing air rifle, and three-position small-bore.

Other Marksmanship Programs for Civilians

Aside from the official government-chartered CMP, there are a few other associations that offer marksmanship events and grading.

Project Appleseed was founded in 2006 by the Revolutionary War Veterans Association. Shooting on the "Quick and Dirty" Appleseed QAT, those scoring 210 or higher out of 250 earn themselves the designation of Rifleman and issued with a Rifleman patch. The levels of rating used by Project Appleseed are similar to the United States military marksmanship grading; Unqualified, Marksman, Sharpshooter, and Rifleman replace Expert.

The National Rifle Association of America (NRA) is a non-profit American organization that was founded in 1871. They are responsible for sponsoring marksmanship events that feature skilled shooting and sport.

The Fundamentals of Marksmanship

When it comes to marksmanship, there are several fundamentals to learn. Learning these fundamentals will help you to become a better shooter with greater accuracy. It is imperative that any gun owner who intends to use their firearm, instead of letting it just gather dust, learns these fundamentals. After all, a gun is only as good as its user. If you are unskilled and unfamiliar with the fundamentals of marksmanship, you are not only an ineffective shooter, you are a downright danger to yourself and others. Improper use and handling of firearms account for many grave injuries and even fatalities as a result of accidents.

There are eight fundamentals to handgun shooting. Four of the fundamentals are important for safe shooting at a shooting range. However, the other four are crucial to making the shot. If you have any weaknesses in one of those crucial found fundamentals, it will show in your shooting. One of the reasons many people aren't keen on shooting handguns is that they aren't very successful at making the shot and, let's face it, there is no enjoyment in shooting if you can't successfully hit your target.

Many people can't name, in order, the fundamentals of shooting a handgun. If you aren't familiar with the fundamentals, you can't pinpoint the areas in which you need improvement. If you can't discern where you need to improve, you can't work at getting better and you will never make that shot. If you can't make the shot on the range, you have no chance of making the shot in a life and death self-defense situation. As they say, "Practice makes perfect," and it is especially applicable to handgun shooting. Practicing and mastering the fundamentals will allow you to accurately make the shot every time and stand out of the crowd instead of just being an average shooter which may be important to those wanting to shoot competitively.

Important note: Each person is unique, built differently, may have injuries, etc. The guidelines detailed below for the fundamentals of handgun shooting are only that; guidelines. While certain stances, for instance, are proven to be optimal across the board, not everyone can strictly adopt a stance according to the guidelines and maintain it comfortably. Comfort is an important aspect of shooting. If you are not comfortable, your shooting accuracy will suffer. It is important to take stock of the guidelines and to then make slight, reasonable adjustments to suit your physical makeup or any injuries.

Stance or Position

Your stance or position relates mainly to situations when you are able to adopt a position similar to the one you would use while shooting at a firing range. In reality, however, things could be very different as you may be kneeling or even lying down on your stomach while taking cover in the face of a shootout.

Isosceles or Modified Isosceles

The most popular and effective shooting stance is called the Isosceles or Modified Isosceles stance. It was popularized in the 1980s when Rob Leatham and Brian Enos started employing the stance to win at International Practical Shooting Confederation competitions. It is now acknowledged as one of two main handgun shooting stances. This stance gets its name from the isosceles triangle in geometry in which the triangle has two of its three sides that are of equal length. Translating this into handgun shooting, it refers to a position in which both arms are held straight out forward in front of the body which makes both arms equal in length. A modification to this stance is to bend one or both arms slightly which may help accommodate your individual body makeup and make the stance more comfortable to maintain.

- Stand facing your target squarely, be sure not to be angling your body or torso to one side or the other.
- Lock both arms straight out in front of your torso, or employ the modification of bending your arms slightly.
- Stand with both feet planted firmly on the ground, approximately shoulder-width apart.
- Lean your shoulders slightly forward of your hips.
- Keep your knees slightly bent.

It is important to lean slightly forward in this position. Leaning forward shifts your center of gravity forward which helps you better control the recoil of your firearm when firing a shot. You can tell if you are standing too straight and need to lean more forward if your toes are lifting off the ground from the recoil. Adjust the amount you are leaning forward in small increments to find the position that works best for you.

The advantages of the isosceles position include:
- It is a natural position and can therefore be sustained more easily.
- It allows your torso to turn 180 degrees.
- It provides a solid, stable base while shooting.

- The shoulders and torso face the target squarely which presents a possible shooter with the strongest part of any type of body armor you may be wearing.
- It allows you to draw your weapon efficiently.
- It allows you to move out of the way or react to the actions of your target easily.

Weaver Stance

The weaver is the second of the two most popular handgun shooting stances and closely resembles the isosceles stance with a few notable differences. The weaver stance was developed by a Los Angeles County Deputy Sheriff, Jack Weaver, in the 1950s. The aim was to help him win "leather slap" pistol shooting competitions in Southern California. In these competitions, quick draw shooting was the name of the game and often involved a non-sighted shooting from the hip technique. However, Weaver wanted to develop a quick draw technique whereby he could use the gun's sights by drawing it to eye-level for superior accuracy in competition.

The weaver stance adopts a traditional boxing of fighting stance which allows you to not only shoot but also to move, change position, kick, or even throw a punch easily from the same position.

- Stand with your feet planted firmly on the ground shoulder-width apart.
- Step slightly back with your dominant foot or the foot on the same side to the hand you hold the firearm in. This should be a comfortable stance with the front and back foot placed not too far apart.
- The toes of the forward, non-dominant, foot should be pointing forward, toward the target. The toes of the backward, dominant, leg can be facing forward to angled out to the side but not more than 45 degrees.

- Maintain a lateral distance of shoulder-width between the two feet even though one is placed more forward and the other more backward.

- Bend both knees somewhat. The knee of the forward leg will be bent more while the knee of the backward leg. This will allow the forward, non-dominant, leg support more of the shooter's weight than the backward leg. The knee of the backward leg will be straighter than the forward leg but do not lock out the backward knee.

- This position will naturally allow the shooter to lean forward from the hips, leaning the shoulders forward until your nose is almost in line with the toes of your forward leg.

- Both arms will be extended out from your body but not in the same position as with the isosceles stance. Instead of both arms being of equal length, in the weaver stance, the arms will be at different lengths. Both hands will be holding the gun with the dominant arm being held straight out or with a very slight bend in the elbow. The supporting arm will have a noticeable bend in the elbow with the elbow down toward the ground. This will draw your shoulders in toward each other slightly and angle the supporting arm's shoulder slightly toward the dominant, shooting arm. This is different from the isosceles stance in that your torso is not facing the target completely squarely.

The arm position of the weaver stance provides the shooter with a push and pull action. While the shooting arm pushes forward, the supporting arm pulls backward. This helps provide more stable aiming and increased muzzle control.

Grip

Your grip on your gun is established while the firearm is still in its holster. From the moment you draw your weapon to the moment that you re-holster it, your grip should remain unchanged. Consistency is key to becoming a skilled shooter. Every aspect of shooting should stay the same whether it's your stance, grip, draw, etc. If you keep switching up how you do any of the fundamentals of marksmanship, you will not get consistent results and you cannot possibly hope to improve. Not even constant practice will help you to perfect your shooting skill if you aren't practicing in exactly the same way in everything you do. One of the most important things a consistent grip helps you achieve is consistent and improved recoil management. Different gun grips produce different recoil actions. Learning to manage recoil requires you to have consistency in the recoil. If the recoil is always different, you cannot learn to manage it. One of the most important factors of consistent recoil is that it allows you to get a second sight picture more quickly and that gives you a better recovery.

Important note: For grip description, the dominant hand will be the right hand and the supporting hand will be the left hand, presuming that the shooter is right-handed.

Pistol Grip

- Looking at your right hand, the webbed section between your thumb and forefinger creates a V. Place this V high up on the firearm's backstrap or the back of the grip but not so high that it would be in the way of the slide when firing.
- Wrap the last three fingers around the bottom of the gun grip, below the trigger guard. That is the middle, ring, and little finger of your right hand.
- Allow the index or pointer finger of your right hand to remain straight along the barrel of the gun, away from the trigger. Do not ever wrap your trigger finger around the trigger unless you are preparing to definitely shoot your target. Finger off the trigger until you are ready to pull it.
- Wrap the thumb of your right hand around the gun, below the slide, and straight along the other side of the gun barrel.

- Take your left hand and wrap all fingers except your thumb around the gun grip and over the top of your right hand's fingers. The index finger of your left hand should be wrapped over the middle finger of your right hand. The thumb of your left hand should come to rest along the gun barrel below the thumb of your right hand. The heel of your left palm should be resting against the gun grip, almost in line with the heel of your right-hand palm on the other side. If the heel of your left palm is much further forward than that of your right hand, your grip is incorrect and you need to bring your left hand further back along with the gun so that it rests on the side of the gun grip.

This is what is known as the "thumbs straight" grip and is the most successful grip used by serious shooters.

Revolver Grip

- Using your dominant hand, place the V web between the thumb and index finger high up on the grip of the revolver with the thumb wrapped around the other side of the firearm and curled to point downward.
- Using that same hand, wrap the middle finger, ring finger, and little finger around the handle of the revolver with the middle finger resting against the underside of the firearm's trigger guard.
- The index finger or trigger finger on your dominant hand should be resting straight against the frame, below the cylinder.
- Place your supporting hand on the other side of the revolver, the heel of your supporting hand in line with the heel of your dominant hand.
- Wrap the fingers of your supporting hand around the fingers of your dominant hand with the index finger resting under the trigger guard.

- Curl your supporting hand's thumb over the thumb of your dominant hand, pointing downward.

Grip Mistakes to Avoid

Most grip mistakes cause a loss of accuracy when firing a shot. Here are some of the common mistakes made when gripping a firearm which leads to a lack of control while firing.

- Loose wrists allow the gun to move around before or as the shot is being fired. You must be able to hold the gun completely still in order to successfully and accurately make the shot. Hold your wrists as if they are a vice on the firearm to prevent unnecessary movement and loss of accuracy.
- Not using your supporting hand correctly affects accuracy in that you are not able to keep the firearm still. Sure, shooting single-handed in Hollywood blockbusters looks really cool but it's not practical at all in real life. For one, the recoil would be almost completely unmanageable. Using your supporting hand to properly support your dominant shooting hand will help to make your aim more accurate and help you to return the gun to the target more quickly after firing a shot. One of the first ways to tell that you are not properly supporting your dominant hand with your supporting hand happens when the gun is fired. If your grip and hands come apart, either completely or partially to some degree, when firing a shot, you need to correct how you are using your supporting hand.
- A loose grip on your gun will allow it to move unnecessarily which affects both accuracy and how quickly you can recover your grip after recoil to aim for a second shot. The more tightly you grip the gun, the less it will move around. A rule of thumb might be to grip the gun as if your life depends on it because it just might in a self-defense situation.

- Gripping the gun too low will compromise accuracy when the weapon is fired. Gripping too low offers the gun more movement when firing. Be sure to grip the gun as high as possible so that your thumbs and index trigger finger are almost in line with the barrel. However, do not grip the weapon so high that your hand gets caught by the slide as that could cause injury and permanent damage.

- Using your weaker hand to grip the gun with your stronger hand acting as the supporting hand can be detrimental to your use of a firearm. Always ensure that your dominant hand is gripping the gun while your weaker hand is wrapped over the dominant hand for a two-handed grip.

- Crossing your thumbs around the firearm while gripping it is putting your hands at increased risk of injury from the slide as it moves backward while firing. Sometimes this may cause minor injury, at others it could cause serious injury.

Drawing

When push comes to shove and you are faced with an attacker pointing a firearm at you, even from a distance, you have to decide whether you can draw quickly enough to shoot first or not. The further you are away from the assailant, the better your chances but it is still a life and death decision. If your attacker has a weapon in hand but hasn't yet raised it to aim, your decision remains the same. Drawing your weapon is as important as any other of the fundamentals of marksmanship.

Drawing a firearm may seem, to the layperson, to be a safe part of self-defense. However, the reality is far from that. It is one of the most possibly dangerous aspects of handling a gun. Drawing is one of the most visible and noticeable elements of self-defense. While you are drawing your firearm, you are giving your attacker the most visual cue that you are about to retaliate while leaving yourself open and vulnerable to them making the first move and firing the first shot. As stated before, guns are effective deadly weapons even at long range. For that reason, you need to be well-practiced at effectively drawing your weapon quickly. You have to be confident in your ability to be a fast draw. You also have to make the decision whether you have a reasonable chance of doing so without the attacker firing first and mortally wounding you. This is why drawing your weapon takes proper technique and then practice, practice, practice to perfect it.

The common drawing of a firearm travels in a straight, diagonal line in an upward trajectory. However, this presents two problems. Firstly, your firearm is not in a good position until your arm is fully extended. Even if your arm is fully extended, if your attacker is in close proximity, you cannot effectively engage in a shootout. Secondly, in small spaces, behind the steering wheel of your car, for instance, the likelihood of your weapon hitting an obstruction and not being drawn in a smooth motion is pretty good which would make your draw ineffective to preempt your attacker's response to your draw.

The traditional draw method has been losing favor for several years in the wake of a newer method of drawing your weapon, a right-angled technique. This is often called a tight quarters draw or a close-quarters draw. Let's explore both methods.

Close Quarters Draw

Using the close quarters draw, you should assume your preferred shooting stance. It is also a good idea to practice this draw in a variety of situations, such as seated in a vehicle or in other positions where assuming a traditional shooting stance isn't possible.

With the close quarters draw, the gun is angled toward the target the moment it leaves the holster. The firearm is brought upward along the side of your chest and ribcage. This is where it meets your supporting hand and then is extended toward the target as far as is necessary to make the shot but the shot can effectively be taken as soon as the gun is just out of the holster. For any drawing technique, a good and proper grip on the firearm is crucial to hitting your target.

The firearm should be gripped as high as possible to the slide with your V-webbing between thumb and index finger being placed in line with your arm's skeletal structure. The high placement on the gun's grip ensures better recoil control. Grasp the gun tightly. Your middle finger should be tightly pressed in an upward position under the trigger guard. The thumb of your hand should be held along the side or frame of the barrel of the gun, pointed at your target.

Bringing your support hand up at the same time as this dominant hand drawing motion is happening, you will achieve a two-handed grip shortly after drawing your weapon. Your trigger finger should be tightly pressed against the side of the firearm in an upward motion directly under the trigger guard. The thumb grip should be the same with the "thumbs straight" as detailed above with thumbs pointing at your target.

Use your supporting hand to not only stabilize the gun but also strengthen your grip on the gun using your supporting hand so that you can more effectively control the recoil. To do this, use your supporting hand to tighten the grip of your dominant hand by squeezing your hand. Once the firearm has cleared any obstructions, angle and aim it at your target. Slide the gun upward along your ribs and across your chest before extending your arms to hold the gun out in front of you.

The importance of a proper grip cannot be stressed enough. Trying to re-grip your firearm after you've drawn it almost never works and you cannot shoot accurately if you don't start out with a good grip.

As with all over aspects of marksmanship, the drawing takes practice. When you get the close quarters draw correct, you will notice that the gun is ready to fire from the moment it leaves the holster and you've angled it upward toward your intended target. It is also ready to be fired along the entire path from your hip, up along your body, and into full extension out in front of you.

Caution: While this draw is safe to practice and use, shooting without using the sight of your firearm shouldn't be attempted by a novice. You should have practiced and gained proficiency in shooting from the hip if you intend to use this draw and possibly fire before the firearm is at full extension. If you are not proficient, you could miss your target, giving them the opportunity to shoot you, but you could also shoot a non-target in the process.

Standard Draw

Assume your preferred stance with the bottom half of your body.

While reaching for your firearm grip with your dominant hand, bring the supporting hand up to about your solar plexus or just below chest height. Don't leave your supporting hand dangling limply at your side. When you are drawing your weapon, get into the habit of moving your supporting hand at the same time as you move your dominant hand.

While moving to draw your firearm, keep your eyes locked on your target. It's no use looking down at your firearm and losing sight of a potential target or threat. This will leave you vulnerable to the actions of a would-be attacker.

As you bring the gun up to solar plexus height, put your supporting hand in place to create the "thumbs straight" grip with your dominant hand's thumb just below the trigger. Once a two-handed grip on the gun is established at solar plexus height, you push the firearm away from your body, extending your arms outwards toward your target, and disengage the safety as you do so.

Bringing the gun up to eye level, you get sight alignment and sight picture, moving your dominant hand's index finger onto the trigger as you do so, ready to fire.

Sight Alignment and Sight Picture

Sight alignment is when the front sight is evenly spaced within the rear sight and is level at the top of the rear sight.

The sight picture is when the front sight is in the center of the target's mass, evenly spaced within the rear sight, and is level at the top of the rear sight. The front sight should be completely clear while the target behind it should be out of focus or fuzzy.

For a sight picture, the target must be out of focus because the human eye can't simultaneously focus on two subjects at varying distances from each other. One of the two subjects will be out of focus. To make the shot, your front sight must be in focus and you must know where it is aimed in relation to your target. You will still be able to see your target, even if it is out of focus.

Some people find difficulty making the shot with a handgun because they don't make sure that the front sight is clearly in focus, they focus instead on the target. Without a proper sight alignment and a clear sight picture, while the target is out of focus, you can very easily miss the target, even at close range. Again, consistency is key. You must ensure proper alignment and a clear sight picture with every shot you take. It's not going to do much good to have a clear sight picture for one shot and not have it for the next shot, your results will be as inconsistent as your sight picture.

What about the dots? This may seem strange but when using your front sight in daylight conditions, don't use the dots. Why? The dots are there for low light conditions where you can't properly see where the front sight is in relation to the rear sight for sight alignment. In darker conditions, you can use the dots to see where the front sight is in relation to the rear sight by making sure that the front sight dot is evenly spaced between and level with the rear dots.

Breathing

Nobody thinks about breathing properly in a life or death self-defense situation. It's a given. There are so many other things to think about in those moments that it's easy to neglect your breathing but proper breathing could make a world of difference. Adrenaline is released into your bloodstream when the fight or flight instinct kicks in. When your fight or flight instinct kicks in and adrenaline floods your system, You will find yourself taking quicker, shallower breaths or even holding your breath which could deprive your body of much-needed oxygen in those moments. You may not have the luxury of time to employ a breathing exercise to achieve optimal proper breathing but there is something you can do. You need to take deep breaths to keep a steady oxygen flow in your bloodstream. After all, your brain won't function nearly as well if it is lacking oxygen and in panic mode at the same time.

Should you not be in a self-defense situation, learning to breathe properly can't do any harm and it's more than likely to improve your marksmanship. Breathing in increased the amount of air in your lungs, inflating them, and increasing the pressure in your chest. This is what makes your chest expand and lift upward. Exhaling decreases the pressure, allowing your chest to contract and fall lower. How does this affect your use of a firearm?

When your chest rises and falls, your gun moves, and making a shot accurately becomes more difficult. Keeping your breathing uniform and consistent helps to keep your shots on target. While breathing, both your body and your firearm will keep moving. By controlling your breathing, your ability to keep your firearm steady increases.

Breathing deeply and slowly is more conducive to maintaining your blood oxygen level than shorter, shallower breaths. When you take short, shallow breaths, you increase the frequency with which your chest and shoulders move. It's also not good for keeping a steady supply of oxygen entering your body. Breathing deeply and rhythmically is also calming to the mind which improves your concentration and muscle tension.

Another aspect of controlled breathing is that it's not only about breathing deeply and rhythmically. It's about your breathing technique. If you aren't familiar with belly breathing, simply taking a deep breath will cause your chest to expand and rise, in which case deep breathing will be of no use at all. You need to learn to breathe into your stomach and not your chest in order to keep your chest and shoulders as still as possible.

Observe how your breathing affects your aim, even with a handgun. Stretch your arms out in front of you as if holding a firearm and take a few breaths. Notice how much movement you are getting as your chest and shoulders rise and fall with each breath.

Ideally, you should learn to breathe into your stomach; however, you can use another method to help you stabilize your upper body while taking a shot.

Relaxed Shot

- Begin by breathing normally while you assume your preferred shooting stance and unholster your gun.
- Raise your gun into the firing position.
- Take a breath and let it out.
- Hold your breath on the exhale for between three to five seconds.
- During this brief period of holding your breath, find your sight alignment and sight picture and squeeze the trigger.

Don't attempt to hold your breath for longer than five seconds in a bid to get a better sight picture. If you can't get it within those few seconds; breathe in, exhale, and try again.

Firing a round during the pauses between breaths gives you greater precision due to your body being in a relaxed state and there being no movement from breathing.

Trigger Control

Trigger control is defined as skillfully manipulating the trigger in order to fire a shot while still maintaining your sight alignment and sight picture.

- Isolate the movement of your trigger finger, do not move any other part of either your dominant or supporting hand.
- Apply even pressure to the trigger, pulling all the way back in a single motion.
- Maintain your sight alignment and sight picture.
- Do not stop the trigger squeeze at any point, pause, or hesitate. Make the squeeze a single, smooth motion.
- Once you have fired the shot, immediately restore sight alignment and sight picture, preparing to fire the next shot off in precisely the same way.

The trigger press is only one part of successful trigger control. The placement of your trigger finger on the trigger and the placement of your index finger of your supporting hand play vital roles in the process. You should place the index finger of your dominant hand, or your trigger finger so that the trigger is positioned about halfway through your fingerprint or halfway between the tip of your finger and the first crease. If you have too much trigger finger on the trigger, or if your finger is too far over the trigger, you risk pulling the firearm toward your dominant side when firing. If there isn't enough trigger finger on the trigger, you risk pushing the firearm off to your non-dominant side when firing. If the index finger of your supporting hand is resting around the trigger guard, you also risk pulling the firearm toward your non-dominant side while taking a shot. Your supporting hand's index finger should be over your dominant hand's middle finger, below the trigger guard.

Follow Through

The follow-through is made up of three stages:

- Keep your eyes on the front sight until the weapon has been discharged.
- Regain both sight alignment and sight picture again after firing and prepare to take the next shot.
- Immediately scan your surroundings for any sign of other potential life-threatening targets.

Your attacking target may need to be shot several times to nullify the threat, whether you injure the target enough to stop the threat or kill them. You may also not have hit your target with the first shot.

Bringing the Fundamentals Together

In order to be a good marksman, you need to perfect each one of the fundamentals and bring them all together for each and every shot you make. If you have a weakness in even one of the fundamentals, your overall accuracy and success will suffer. The only way to get better at shooting is to practice and have patience. You aren't going to master marksmanship overnight. If you find that you work on each of the fundamentals and practice regularly but you are still not seeing an improvement, it's worth getting an expert's opinion. Shooting ranges often offer classes and courses so there should be an authority on the subject at your local shooting range. Consult with an expert and let them observe you while you shoot and offer improvement advice. If you want to be able to shoot accurately and successfully in a self-defense situation, it is imperative that you master the fundamentals of marksmanship before you find yourself in a position where weakness could be the death of you.

Chapter 9:

Firearm Choice and Handling

The firearm you invest in will depend not only on the intended purpose, self-defense for instance but also on your personal preference and how passionate you are about firearms. There is variety in caliber, variety in type, models, and more which plays a big role in what you will eventually purchase.

The Choice of Two

When it comes to handguns, there are two basic, popular, choices. You can choose a revolver or you could opt for a semi-automatic pistol. Revolvers have an air of Old West romanticism about them, making them popular with gun enthusiasts who want more than just a self-protection weapon that will get the job done. Old western films definitely help to propagate the popularity of revolvers—every gun-slinging outlawed bandit, sheriff, and cowboy had one. However, the romanticized version of the Old West as portrayed in old films typically spans from 1850 to the 1910s. The revolver was the handgun available during that time since the first semi-automatic pistol wasn't created until 1896. Today, however, there is a wide variety of firearms to choose from. For self-defense, the most popular choices are revolvers and semi-automatic pistols, each with its own benefits and drawbacks.

Revolvers vs. Semi Automatic Pistols

Revolvers are as good a choice for self-defense and concealed carry as semi-automatic pistols because each one brings its own unique characteristics to the party. Semi-automatic pistols are a very popular choice of handguns today. Unlike the old-fashioned appeal of a revolver, pistols have become synonymous with the modern handgun, especially popularized by modern Hollywood action blockbuster films. The likelihood is good that the younger generations will favor this type of firearm.

Reliability

While revolvers are not infallible to malfunction, in general, they are more reliable than any make or model of semi-automatic available on the market due to their simplistic design. While both revolvers and semi-automatic pistols have moving parts, revolvers have fewer moving parts which reduces the chance of breakage or malfunction. When it comes to owning a handgun for self-defense, no attribute is more important than reliability. You can't defend yourself against an attacker if your gun is broken or malfunctioning. Semi-automatic pistols are much more prone to malfunctions, especially if they are not meticulously maintained.

Resilience and Malfunction

Revolvers may be more resilient in the face of dirt and dust than semi-automatic pistols thanks to their more simplistic design. When the design includes fewer moving parts, there are fewer nooks and crannies that can become clogged up with debris which would cause a malfunction. While revolvers tend to suffer fewer breakages and malfunctions than semi-automatic pistols; when they break, they break spectacularly. While some semi-automatic pistol malfunctions may be correctable by the owner through cleaning and maintenance, most revolver breakages require the intervention of a professional gunsmith.

An example of a very serious malfunction on a revolver is a case of the cylinder locking up and not rotating.

Ease of Use

Aside from reliability, the ease of using a firearm for self-defense is the second most important factor, especially if you are a newcomer to the use of firearms and have never owned or used one before. A revolver has no slide that must be pulled back to cock it in anticipation of firing. All you have to do is open the cylinder, load the rounds, clip the cylinder back into place, use a single-handed action to pull the hammer back and squeeze the trigger. Double action revolvers develop this ease of use even further. Instead of having to cock the hammer for each shot, double-action revolvers use the trigger squeeze to pull the hammer back and at the end of the squeeze the hammer falls and the bullet is fired. This negates having to cock the weapon at all. This may be advantageous in a self-defense situation where you may not have the time to cock a semi-automatic weapon by pulling the slide back to chamber the first round before firing, especially if your target is at close range and could fire first.

However, let's not discount the ease of use perks that semi-automatic pistols offer. The smaller caliber rounds offer less recoil, the designs are usually made to fit more comfortably in the hand, and the trigger is often shorter and lighter to squeeze.

Caliber

In modern times; revolvers are available in a wide variety of calibers. The traditional calibers of revolvers include .357, .38, 41, 44, and larger. However, these days you also have revolvers that take traditional semi-automatic calibers such as 9mm, .40, and 45 in models like the Pitbull and Charter Arms. This means that no matter what caliber you are looking for, you'll likely find it in a revolver option.

Ability to Conceal

Many revolvers are designed to be easy to concealed carry. Some examples include the Smith and Wesson J-Frames, Kimber K6, and the Charter Arms. These revolvers are easy to conceal on your person in a good holster. An additional feature that makes many revolvers easy to conceal is that their small size and lightweight make them comfortable to carry on your person. Even as revolvers get bigger, some people still find them manageable to carry.

Capacity

The biggest drawback to a revolver for self-defense is the limited number of rounds you can load at a time. Many revolvers come with only a six-round capacity which gives you only 6 shots to stop the target. Revolvers do come in capacities of between five and eight rounds but even an eight-round revolver doesn't match the capacity of a semi-automatic pistol. If your attacker isn't killed or severely enough injured to halt the attack, you would need to reload before taking more shots. If you miss shots, that leaves you with fewer shots available without reloading. If you need to take on more than one target in a self-defense confrontation, you need to shoot incredibly accurately to make each shot count. Semi-automatic guns, on the other hand, offer magazines taking between seven and 15 rounds per clip. This is dependent on the size as smaller pistols designed for easier concealed carry take smaller magazines due to their smaller size.

Reloading

When it comes to reloading, semi-automatic pistols are definitely the easier option. You can simply eject the spent clip and slide a full clip into place to continue shooting. When using a revolver; you need to clip the cylinder open, tilt the gun to tip the empty shell casings out, and then manually reload the rounds. There is a device on the market that inserts rounds into the cylinder chambers. This allows you to reload a revolver faster by pushing all the new rounds in at the same time. However, this is not quite as efficient as simply clipping a new magazine into a pistol.

Trigger Squeeze

Double-action revolvers have a long and heavy trigger squeeze as your trigger pulls the hammer back as you squeeze before releasing it at the end of the squeeze. Your trigger squeeze, therefore, needs to be strong and consistent. If you don't pull the trigger back far enough, falter, hesitate, or don't have the hand strength to pull the trigger back all the way, your ability to fire successfully is compromised. The weaker your hand and finger strength, the harder you have to work to squeeze the trigger. Putting more effort into squeezing the trigger could lead to pulling on the trigger instead of just squeezing which could pull the firearm off target.

Safety

Due to the revolver's heavier trigger squeeze, which many would see as a drawback, it could also prove safer in the face of accidental trigger squeeze accidents. It's a fact that it takes more work and strength to squeeze the trigger of a revolver than a semi-automatic pistol. Due to this, you are less likely to be able to accidentally pull the trigger when you don't mean to.

Sight

Revolvers have front and rear sights that are closer together than on traditional semi-automatic firearms. It is often easier for individuals to use a sighting system where the two sights are placed further apart for more accurate shots. A good example is a snub-nosed revolver which has a much shorter barrel and thus the sights are extremely close together, making an inexperienced shooter much less accurate when making the shot.

Weight

Revolvers are often made of heavier and more robust materials such as steel, allowing them to accommodate larger calibers and reduce recoil. However, the tradeoff is that unlike modern semi-automatic pistols which are made of light-weight materials such as polymers, revolvers are often heavier to hold and carry.

Width

The revolving cylinders that revolvers get their name for may make them wider than semi-automatic pistols which are designed to be sleeker. Wider firearms are more difficult to conceal while carrying than sleeker weapons.

Accessories

Modern semi-automatic pistols offer you the option to purchase and add on various accessories and rails, adding to the 'cool' factor and use of the firearm. When it comes to revolvers, however, this isn't the case and there aren't many accessories available for the firearm.

Which is Better?

The answer to that question is entirely subjective. It depends on your personal preference, strength, shape, and size of your hands, and the caliber you are looking to use. Every experienced gun owner or enthusiast will debate the topic until the cows come home, each having their own, personal opinion. However, nobody can make the decision between these two different handgun types for you. What it may come down to is visiting a gun range to pick up, hold, and shoot different caliber weapons, makes, models, sizes, etc. in both types to decide which you prefer.

What to Look for in a Self-Defense Handgun

While both semi-automatic pistols and revolvers can meet each of the following important criteria for a self-defense handgun, it will come down to your personal preference that will dictate which one you choose. That being said, there are specific attributes you must be aware of and look for when choosing a firearm for your personal protection.

Stopping power: Your chosen weapon should have enough power to stop the threat. A small-caliber gun may be lighter and smaller to carry concealed but it may be too small a caliber to really put your target out of action when it comes to a life and death situation.

Round penetration: Your chosen firearm should use ammunition that offers limited penetration. To stop a target doesn't require a shot to be through-and-through so choosing a weapon that won't send a bullet through a wall is a safer choice to limit any possible collateral damage.

Reliability: Your weapon needs to be reliable in a variety of different tactical situations and not prone to jamming or malfunctioning when you need it most. A malfunction at a critical moment could cost you your life.

Easy handling: You need a firearm that is easy to use, points well, fits comfortably in your hand, and is appropriate for your firearm experience level.

Capacity and reload: The more rounds a firearm holds, the more chances you have to hit your target and stop the threat before having to reload. Reloading should also be an easy and quick process. If you haven't stopped the threat within the number of rounds your weapon holds, you may not have the time to reload it.

Accuracy: A well-made, quality firearm will be more accurate than a cheaper alternative. That being said, a gun that is too heavy will tax your arms when aiming and that could put your accuracy off as well.

Both the handler and the gun must be able to work well together in order to stay on target.

When investing in a firearm, it is worthwhile doing your homework before you even set foot in a gun shop or anywhere that legally sells firearms. You should familiarize yourself with makes and models of both revolvers and semi automatic handguns so that you have a greater understanding and idea of what it is that you are in the market for. It's never a bad idea to approach an authority on firearms and their use for self-defense. You can get some good advice from a qualified instructor offering certified firearms training courses. While their advice will be subjective to their own, personal preferences, they will give you greater insight for making your decision. Don't simply walk into a gun dealer and ask the clerk behind the counter for advice. While they may be knowledgeable, they may not be qualified to give the best possible advice or an authority on the matter. Once you have armed yourself with all the necessary information, approach a dealer, and ask to see the makes and models of firearms you have singled out as possible candidates. Ask the dealer for permission to handle each weapon and perform a dry fire. This will allow you to get a feel for how the gun fits in your hand, the weight, and the effort necessary to pull the trigger. Remember how revolvers take more effort to pull the trigger than semi automatic pistols? You need to find a gun that is suitable, easy enough to use, and isn't too heavy. It's like trying on clothes before you buy them. If you don't try them on, you may be disappointed if they don't fit you properly when you get home. The same principle applies to purchasing firearms. If you think that you have found a good match, that's great! If the dealer doesn't have anything that really feels right, don't make a purchase simply to walk out with a gun. Spend some time shopping around to find the best gun for your needs. Don't just take the first available option because you want a gun and that's the first available option.

Firearm Operations

There are several differences between the operations of semi-automatic pistols and revolvers. It's important to understand the basic operations of your firearm, build familiarity with your weapon, and become more comfortable handling it efficiently.

Loading and Unloading

Both revolvers and semi-automatic pistols need to be loaded and unloaded with ammunition but the processes are very different for each one.

Revolvers

The classic concept of a revolver is that the cylinder rotates out to the side for loading and reloading but that isn't necessarily always the case. There are various different types of cylinders that need to be loaded and unloaded using methods specific to the type of cylinder.

Front-loading Cylinder

The first revolvers created had front-loading cylinders which may also be referred to as muzzle-loading. They resembled muskets where the powder and rounds were loaded into the weapon separately. Early revolvers were "cap and ball" or caplock weapons due to the compact nature of the caplock method of reloading which made revolvers practical. The weakness of a front-loading cylinder revolver is that it was susceptible to chain firing. The heated gas let off while during a shot would ignite the powder in other chambers within the cylinder. Users also had to tip the revolver vertically after each shot fired to expel the pieces of the percussion cap to fall out otherwise there was a risk of them entering the weapon's mechanism and causing it to jam.

Loading a front-loading cylinder was a time-consuming practice and often awkward, making it impossible to use the weapon effectively in the heat of conflict.

Fixed Cylinder

Early cartridge cylinder revolvers were reloaded by removing the base pin, which allowed the cylinder to revolve and removing the cylinder completely to reload the rounds. Most of these revolvers were single-action weapons. Some modern "micro revolvers" utilizing a small caliber such as .22, make use of this removable cylinder design. These revolvers don't have the necessary stopping power to stop an attacker in their tracks but they are easy to conceal due to their small size, being small enough that they fit into the palm of your hand.

Later single-action revolvers were created with a fixed cylinder in which a loading gate located at the rear of the weapon is used for reloading. This method allowed only one cartridge to be loaded at a time.

Top-Break Cylinder

Top-break revolvers have a hinged frame at the front bottom of the cylinder. Unloading and reloading for these firearms involve releasing the locking mechanism and pushing the barrel of the gun downward to expose the back of the cylinder. Performing this action activates an extractor which pushes the spent cartridges out of the chambers far enough to simply fall out or be easily removed by hand. New rounds can then be put into the cylinder after which the cylinder and barrel are lifted and locked back into place, ready to shoot. The reloading method of top-break revolvers allows quicker reloading than for fixed frame revolvers. This design is almost obsolete in modern times.

Tip-up Cylinder

Tip-up revolvers are designed to use metallic rounds and the barrel of the firearm pitched up with a hinge on the front end of the top strap. These Smith and Wesson models had a barrel release mechanism on either side of the frame, forward of the trigger. This design has been continued.

Swing-out Cylinder

The swing-out cylinder revolver is the most modern unloading and loading method for revolvers. The cylinder swings out sideways and downward from the frame, exposing the back of the cylinder. The cylinder has a pivot mount located parallel to the chambers. The cylinder typically swings out to the left in most models and an extractor ejects all cartridges from the cylinder at the same time. Swing-out revolvers can be loaded manually, inserting a single round at a time, or using a speed loader before the cylinder is pushed back in place and the weapon is ready to fire.

The weakness of swing-out revolvers is the crane or the pivot supporting the cylinder. If you employ the flip-out method of swinging the cylinder out without touching it, often portrayed in movies, and then flicking it back into place can bend the pivot with time. When the pivot is bent, the cylinder is pushed out of alignment with the barrel. When the barrel and chambers aren't aligned properly, it can hamper the round's transition from the chamber into the barrel which increases the pressure in the chamber. The weapon then has the potential to explode if a round becomes lodged in the chamber and doesn't fire when struck by the hammer.

Another potential problem with the crane is that the cylinder is only held in place in a closed position at one point at the back of the cylinder. Some modern models have an additional locking latch to offer more support to keep the cylinder in a closed position. The forces exerted during firing can place stress on the crane, weakening it over time.

Unloading and Reloading Swing-Out Cylinder Revolvers

As swing-out revolvers are the most popular design today, the method of reloading them is the most common to be practiced.

- Open the cylinder by using your right thumb to release the latch on the left side of the revolver. At the same time, use your left hand to cup the gun.
- As the cylinder swings out, push your left hand's two middle fingers through the fame while maintaining a secure grip on the gun and ensure that the cylinder has swung all the way out.
- Tip the revolver's muzzle upward with your two middle fingers still in place, holding the cylinder in the open position. It is impossible for the gun to fire when the cylinder is all the way out.
- Gravity will do the work and the spent cartridges will simply fall out of the chambers provided the gun is held completely vertically, muzzle facing upward.
- As you tilt the revolver upward, close your cupped left hand around the cylinder to prevent it from rotating.
- Use the heel of your palm to hit the extractor rod, only once and relatively sharply so that it goes down all the way. Avoid using your thumb to hit the extractor rod as it may be painful and not strong enough to get the job done if there is a casing lodged in a chamber.
- **Do not** strike the ejector rod multiple times, juggle it, or repeatedly strike it only halfway down.
- While the cylinder is fully open, inspect it to make sure that the gun is fully unloaded.
- With the cylinder still fully open, place the butt of the gun against your body. If you are in the face of danger, this will allow you to feel your way through reloading and keep your eyes on the target. It will also be helpful if you are reloading in low light or dark conditions.
- Make sure that the revolver is held completely vertically with the muzzle pointing straight down toward the ground. This way gravity will help you simply drop the new rounds into the chambers.

- Before inserting the new rounds, wrap your left hand entirely around the cylinder so that the fingers replace your right hand's middle fingers in the frame, supporting the cylinder. You can then use your free right hand to insert the rounds manually, one-by-one, or use a speed loader
- If using a speed loader, use your thumb and index finger to guide two rounds in alignment with the chambers which will put it in the correct position for reloading.
- Don't force the rounds into the cylinder, allow them to be guided in while gently wiggling the loader in a downward motion.
- When the rounds are in place, twist the handle of the speed loader to release them.
- Using your left hand, swing the cylinder back into place as you move your right hand into a shooting position. Give the cylinder a little wiggle with your left hand to ensure it is properly in place before moving your left hand into the shooting position along with your right hand.

Unloading and Reloading Semi-Automatic Pistols

Unloading a pistol may be done to make it safe for storage. A pistol ejects the spent shell casings as a shot is fired. Unlike a revolver, you won't need to unload spent shell casings before you can reload the weapon.

Unloading
- Point the muzzle of the gun in a safe direction so that you don't shoot yourself or a non-target if the gun accidentally discharges.
- If the safety is not on and you can reload the firearm with the safety on, switch it on.

- Ensure that you keep all fingers outside the trigger guard to avoid a potential accidental discharge in case of there being a chambered round and the safety fails.
- Release the magazine and remove it from the pistol.
- Take all of the cartridges out of the magazine.
- Rack the slide by pulling it all the way back toward the rear of the firearm which will eject a chambered round if there is one. Rack the slide a couple of times to be completely sure that the chamber is empty
- Visually check that the chamber and magazine is completely empty.

Emergency Reload/Normal Reload

An emergency reload, or ER can be done when all rounds have been spent and there isn't a round left to be chambered and fired.

- When all the rounds have been spent, the firearm's slide will lock back in an open position which indicates that the gun has run out of ammunition.
- Point the firearm in a safe direction to avoid shooting a non-target, or yourself, if there is an accidental discharge.
- Hold the firearm in your dominant hand so that you can reload with your supporting hand.
- Press the magazine release to eject the empty magazine and remove it.
- Holding the new magazine in your supporting hand, use your supporting hand's index finger as a guide when inserting.
- Ensure that the magazine is firmly locked in place before pulling the slide backward and releasing it forward.

Speed Reload

A speed reload, or SR, can be performed when the magazine is not completely empty and there is a chambered round in the firearm and it is still in battery (ready to fire). This is a method that should only be employed in a life or death situation where there is a pause or lull in the threat and where you don't have time to perform an emergency or normal reload. The partially spent magazine is allowed to fall to the ground after it is ejected. Allowing the magazine to drop to the ground saves you time as you don't have to fumble to remove and pocket it.

- Point the muzzle of the firearm in a safe direction to avoid accidentally shooting a non-target. Remember, there is a chambered round in the gun and if there is any accidental manipulation of the trigger it will fire.

- Hold the gun high, about where the middle of your chest is, just below your chin. This will allow you to scan your surroundings while reloading and use your peripheral vision to detect movement from potential targets. If there is movement from a threat, there is still a round in the chamber that can be fired before inserting the new magazine. With the firearm still in battery, you don't have to fumble with the slide either after reloading.

- Press the magazine release using the thumb of your dominant hand to eject the magazine.

- Ejecting the magazine can be done single-handed with your dominant hand. While you are pressing the magazine release, use your supporting hand to grab a full magazine.

- Place the elbow of your dominant arm, holding the firearm, against your ribcage for stability, angling the firearm upward which is generally a safe direction unless you are inside a building.

- Place the index finger of your supporting hand holding the new magazine right alongside the strap of the magazine so that it can guide the magazine into place. The tip of your index finger should be resting on the top round in the fresh magazine.

- Put the back of the magazine into the magazine well with the bullet tips facing the front of the gun and ensure that the magazine is locked in place.
- Use your supporting hand to quickly rack the slide, ejecting the chambered round and chambering the first round of the new magazine.

Tactical Reload

A tactical reload, or TR, is similar to a speed reload except that the partially spent magazine is kept for possible later use if needed. This method of reloading takes a great deal of dexterity and fine motor skills and you will have two magazines in your supporting hand at the same time. It is important not to drop on or both of the magazines as it will cost you time to retrieve them. Be sure not to insert the partially spent magazine instead of the full magazine.

- Point the muzzle of the firearm in a safe direction to avoid accidentally shooting a non-target. Remember, there is a chambered round in the gun and if there is any accidental manipulation of the trigger it will fire.
- Before performing any other step of reloading, get the new magazine out and firmly held in your supporting hand between your thumb and index finger, moving to the magazine well.
- Hold the gun high, about where the middle of your chest is, just below your chin. This will allow you to scan your surroundings while reloading and use your peripheral vision to detect movement from potential targets. If there is movement from a threat, there is still a round in the chamber that can be fired before inserting the new magazine. With the firearm still in battery, you don't have to fumble with the slide either after reloading.

- Place the elbow of your dominant arm, holding the firearm, against your ribcage for stability, angling the firearm upward which is generally a safe direction unless you are inside a building.
- Press the magazine release to eject the partially spent magazine, catching it in your supporting hand and placing it between either your two middle fingers or your ring finger and little finger.
- Still holding the full magazine between the thumb and index finger of your supporting hand, insert it into the magazine well with your index finger right alongside the front, and fingertip on the top bullet, to guide it into place.
- Pocket the partially spent magazine.
- Rack your slide to eject the chambered round and chamber a round from the new magazine.

Reload with Retention

When performing a reload with retention or RR, you retain the partially spent magazine for later use if necessary. You don't let the magazine fall to the ground. However, unlike a tactical reload, you first eject and pocket the partially spent magazine and then replace it with the full magazine. Again, for this reloading method, the firearm remains in battery with a chambered round.

- Point the muzzle of the firearm in a safe direction to avoid accidentally shooting a non-target. Remember, there is a chambered round in the gun and if there is any accidental manipulation of the trigger it will fire.
- Hold the gun high, about where the middle of your chest is, just below your chin. This will allow you to scan your surroundings while reloading and use your peripheral vision to detect movement from potential targets. If there is movement from a threat, there is still a round in the chamber that can be

fired before inserting the new magazine. With the firearm still in battery, you don't have to fumble with the slide either after reloading.

- Place the elbow of your dominant arm, holding the firearm against your ribcage for stability and angle the firearm upward (which is generally a safe direction unless you are inside a building).
- Eject the partially spent magazine into your supporting hand and pocket it.
- Grab a new magazine with your supporting hand and, using the index finger to guide it in, insert the magazine into the magazine well, and ensure that it is properly locked in place.
- Rack the slide to eject the chambered round and chamber a round from the new magazine.

Racking

Racking a firearm means pulling the slide all the way back and releasing it again. This can be done to eject a chambered round or, if there isn't a round in the chamber already, to chamber a round from the magazine. It is a vitally important function that all gun owners and users need to learn to do and to do it easily, quickly, and well. There are two methods of racking a semi-automatic pistol.

Slingshot Method

- Hold the firearm slightly above waist-height and relatively close to your body. Having the firearm closer to your body will offer you more leverage for the pulling action. Avoid extending your arms away from your body as this lessens the leverage.
- Grasp the gun with your dominant hand as you would for firing, with your index finger straight out along the frame, outside the trigger guard.

- Point the muzzle of the pistol in a safe direction.
- Ensure that the barrel ejection point is upright, as it would be for firing a gun.
- Pinch the slide on the serrations at the back using your supporting hand's thumb and index finger. The webbing between the two fingers should be behind the slide and not on top of it.
- Rotate the firearm slightly to the left as you pinch the slide. Ensure that you have a good grasp on either side of the slide and that you are grasping a good length of the slide to offer you more control.
- Quickly and firmly pull the slide backward to the full extent as if you were pulling back on a slingshot.
- At the same time you are pulling the slide back with your supporting hand, use your dominant hand to push the firearm forward strongly as if punching forward.
- Once the slide has been pulled all the way back, release it quickly so that it snaps back into place.
- The main function of your supporting hand is to keep the firearm steady, not to only pull the slide back. Your dominant hand should do most of the work of pushing the pistol forward.

This is a fast method of racking your firearm because the gun can remain pointed at the target. When you rotate the firearm back into a fully upright position, your supporting hand can simply slide back into position for a two-handed firing grip. From a self-defense perspective, the slingshot method of racking your gun leaves you more vulnerable to a gun grab.

Over the Top Method

- Hold the firearm slightly above waist-height and relatively close to your body. Having the firearm closer to your body will offer you more leverage for the pulling action. Avoid extending your arms away from your body as this lessens the leverage.

- Grasp the gun with your dominant hand as you would for firing, with your index finger straight out along the frame, outside the trigger guard.
- Point the muzzle of the pistol in a safe direction.
- Ensure that the barrel ejection point is upright, as it would be for firing a gun.
- Use your supporting hand to grasp the slide with the palm of your hand placed over the top of the back of the slide and the heel of your hand resting or pressing against the left side serrations.
- Your supporting hand thumb should be to the back of the slide, but not grasping it, and your other four fingers should be on the right.
- Ensure that no part of your hand or fingers covers any part of the barrel ejection port.
- Rotate the gun slightly to the left.
- Use your supporting hand to steady the weapon and pull backward, punch the firearm forward with your dominant hand so that the slide is pulled all the way back.
- Once the slide has been pulled all the way back, release it quickly so that it snaps back into place.
- While using the over the top method of racking, be sure not to point your firearm significantly toward your supporting side. Keep it pointing forward while facing a safe direction.

While this method if racking isn't as quick as the slingshot method, it offers you a firmer, more powerful grip on the slide.

Locking Back

Being able to lock your slide back or in a position where the barrel ejection port is open is an important function as it allows you to visually inspect the barrel.

- Hold the firearm slightly above waist-height and relatively close to your body. Having the firearm closer to your body will offer you more leverage for the pulling action. Avoid extending your arms away from your body as this lessens the leverage.
- Grasp the gun with your dominant hand as you would for firing, with your index finger straight out along the frame, outside the trigger guard. Place your thumb on the slide locking lever and push upward. It won't go anywhere while the slide is in place but it will move upward once the slide is pulled back.
- Point the muzzle of the pistol in a safe direction.
- Ensure that the barrel ejection point is upright, as it would be for firing a gun.
- Use your supporting hand to grasp the slide with the palm of your hand placed over the top of the back of the slide and the heel of your hand resting or pressing against the left side serrations.
- Your supporting hand thumb should be to the back of the slide, but not grasping it, and your other four fingers should be on the right.
- Ensure that no part of your hand or fingers covers any part of the barrel ejection port.
- Rotate the gun slightly to the left.
- Use your supporting hand to steady the weapon and pull backward, punch the firearm forward with your dominant hand so that the slide is pulled all the way back.
- Once the slide has been pulled all the way back, the slide lock lever will move upward into a designated groove on the slide.
- Ease the slide forward until it is stopped by the slide lock lever.

- When you want to unlock your slide, use the same method as above to pull the slide all the way back. The slide lock will move back down automatically. Release the slide as you would when racking so that it snaps sharply back in place.

Visual Firearm Inspection

To do a full inspection of a firearm would require taking it to pieces as if for cleaning. This requires you to follow the manufacturer's instruction manual on taking the gun apart and putting it back together. However, you can perform a quick visual inspection to ensure that there is no blatant damage or any serious issues with the firearm if it has been in storage for a while or if you are purchasing a new gun.

Ask for Assistance

Checking many parts of a firearm requires you to give them more than just a cursory glance and basic handling. In this case, you may want to ask the owner or retailer for permission and assistance while checking the firearm. In many cases, you will require their permission and if the permission is not given, you may consider why that is. It may be harmless and the owner or retailer simply not wanting to spend the time, especially with retailers where the firearm is brand new in the box. However, if a used firearm is not given the go-ahead to be inspected, there may be a reason, such as a fault that you cannot pick up by simply doing a basic check.

Dry Fire

Performing a dry fire will give you a good indication that the basic function of firing is working properly. When dry firing, check for:

Manually cycle the firearm by performing the action of firing a shot and making sure that all parts work as they should and another shot can be fired immediately after. Rigorous cycling is recommended to ensure that the firearm is ready to fire again and again and not just once as there may be random jamming or other malfunctions that may not occur on the first cycle.

Semi Automatics

- Trigger action should be smooth.
- There should be a smooth slide action that moves all the way backward and all the way back into place in semi-automatic pistols.
- Semi-automatic pistols should go back into battery after a shot is fired.
- The slide should lock back without issues and then the locking mechanism should release automatically and the firearm goes back into battery immediately after.
- Check the trigger reset when the trigger is slowly let out after squeezing.
- Check that the decocker works, if the firearm has one.
- The magazine release should be checked by inserting an empty magazine into the magazine well, ensuring that it doesn't fall out of its own volition and that the release lever works to easily and smoothly eject the magazine.

Revolvers

- Check that the ejector rod on a revolver works correctly.
- Check that a revolver cylinder swings out easily and locks back into place, correctly aligned with the barrel.
- Ensure that the latch holding the cylinder of a revolver works properly to keep the cylinder firmly in place.
- Revolvers should display a smooth cylinder rotation when it is swung out.

- Check that the hammer cocks manually and the cylinder rotates. Check automatic cylinder rotation in double-action revolvers.
- Use dummy rounds.
- When checking that all aspects of the firearm work correctly, not only during a dry fire but also when there is ammunition in the gun, using dummy rounds is a good option to ensure proper chambering of a round in semi-automatic pistols and that the extractor rod works and rounds don't get jammed due to misalignment in revolvers.

Wear and Imperfections

Taking a gun to pieces requires precision and, if you have never done it before, assistance. For new firearms, this isn't strictly necessary but can be useful for familiarizing yourself with the firearm. It is recommended for pre-loved (AKA used) guns as there may be wearing you cannot see from the outside.

- Inspect the barrel for overall condition and rifling. Check for scratches to the barrel and the level of buildup. Scratches to a barrel and affects the accuracy of a firearm. A poorly maintained gun will give you issues down the line.
- Ensure that the feed ramp, opposite the muzzle, is smooth without any dents or gouges. A damaged feed ramp often leads to a feed failure or malfunction.
- Have a close look at the frame and slide. Any burs or metal shavings where the slide makes contact with the frame is a bad sign. Again, check for gouges and imperfections that may be masked by grease. Even new guns may have imperfections from the manufacturing process which a manufacturer may attempt to hide by caking on the grease.
- When reassembling the gun, ensure that all the parts fit back together properly. The slide should match up with the frame

with no side-to-side wiggle. Make sure that all the moving parts of the gun only move in the direction they are intended to move in. Go ahead and give the firearm a good shake to see if you can hear or even feel any rattling of loose pieces.

- Inspect a new or used gun for sight alignment. This is particularly aimed at handguns that have special features to their sights. If a gun has tritium sights, do they still glow? Additionally, check that the sights don't drift in transit. Drifting may occur over time with use.

Check and note the serial number of the firearm you intend to purchase. This isn't really an issue for brand new guys bought from reputable dealers. However, purchasing a used gun, you want to ensure the background is clean and the gun has never been used in a crime or stolen. If the serial number is unreadable or even damaged to obscure it, even if you can make it out, it's a warning sign of someone trying to hide the identity of the gun. If the seller refused to allow you to check the serial number, don't buy the gun. You can find the serial number on the frame, slide, on top of the barrel (perform a slow rack to look for it).

Chapter 10:

Caring for Firearms

Firearm maintenance, also called gun care, is a set of maintenance procedures that all gun owners should be employing to prevent deterioration and maintain the proper function of their firearms.

The Importance of Maintenance

Proper cleaning and care is an important part of being a responsible gun owner. The problem is that far too many gun owners neglect this part of owning a gun in much the same way as they neglect training and practice. It's been mentioned before but it's worth mentioning again. You cannot buy a firearm and simply stash it away in case of emergencies and do absolutely nothing else with it. Just like regular practice will alert you to faulty or worn parts that need replacing, properly maintaining your firearm on a regular basis helps to bolster your weapon against wear and tear and other potential faults that may arise. Rust and debris build up in a firearm over time and not removing it can lead to a failure that puts your life, as well as the lives of others, in danger. Here's why you need to regularly clean and care for your gun.

Accuracy

Accuracy is affected by the buildup of copper fouling inside a firearm. The velocity of the bullet exiting the barrel is decreased and therefore the accuracy is impaired. If you know that your firearm should fire over a distance of 100 yards, copper fouling buildup could decrease that distance by up to half.

Accidents

Accidents that happen due to poor maintenance, such as jamming, are avoidable. If a round jams in the barrel and the handler tries to fire off a second round, the firearm has the potential to explode and grievously injure the handler and any bystanders. A notable example of such an avoidable accident was the death of Bruce Lee's son, Brandon Lee. The firearm was test-fired weeks before it was used in a scene of *The Crow* in 1993. A dummy round got lodged in the barrel and, when used with blanks in the scene, the dummy round was dislodged and fired from the gun, striking Brandon in the abdomen and resulting in his death due to blood loss. Had the firearm been properly maintained and cleaned, the jammed dummy round would have been found and the accident avoided. A catastrophic failure is also possible in the case of extreme buildup inside a guy. The excessive buildup raises the pressure inside the barrel when firing a round. Raising the pressure puts the firearm at risk of exploding, leading to severe injury.

Longevity

Proper maintenance extends a firearm's lifespan. Think about your vehicle, if you do not regularly maintain it, it will eventually become unusable or fall completely apart. This will even happen with vehicles that are not used often. The same principle applies to guns. Regular cleaning removes buildup and rust but also lubricates the gun parts with oil which helps to slow down wear and tear caused by friction between the moving parts. Furthermore, some types of dirt and fouling can actually cause irreparable damage to the gun through corrosion. Regular cleaning will prevent buildup from eating away at your firearm from the inside.

Operational Familiarity

Cleaning and caring for a gun familiarizes the owner with how it operates. To clean and maintain a firearm, it needs to be taken apart. Over time, you will learn exactly how each part fits together and works. Not all guns are created the same and understanding how the mechanisms in your particular gun work give you a better understanding of how to handle it correctly.

Did you know: Guns that utilize a spring to control the dormant state of the firing pin when not in use need the bolt assembly cleaned very regularly to prevent malfunctions such as slam firing.

Who Performs Gun Maintenance?

Firearm maintenance is easy enough for gun owners to perform in the comfort of their own home. You do also have the option of taking your firearm to a gun shop or shooting range where someone with cleaning proficiency will be able to perform maintenance for you. However, it is never a bad idea to learn how to maintain your firearm yourself. Having the ability to perform your own gun maintenance brings you a greater insight into and understanding of the operational functions of your gun.

Maintenance can include a variety of procedures that range from simple to more advanced. Simple methods involve cleaning the gun with cleaning solutions or oil. More advanced methods encompass using grease or oil to lubricate the moving parts and using protective finishes, such as varnish, to recoat surfaces that are exposed.

There are times when a professional gunsmith should be consulted to perform much more advanced maintenance than the owner can perform. Such instances include physical damage to the firearm that affects its ordinary performance or when a potentially life-threatening malfunction is occurring. A professional gunsmith will be able to clean and inspect the firearm to determine whether it can be repaired and whether it is still safe to use. Always consult a professional if you suspect that there is something wrong with your firearm.

All major firearms manufacturing brands will provide an informational manual along with the firearm that details the proper use of the gun, how to disassemble it, proper cleaning methods, and how to put it all back together again. Generally, this manual comes with the firearm when you purchase it. If it is not packaged with the gun upon purchase, you must contact the manufacturer and find out where you can find the information. Always follow the manufacturer's instructions for proper cleaning and maintenance for safe and responsible gun maintenance.

Cleaning Firearms: A Beginner's Crash Course

If you are a new gun owner and you have never cleaned a firearm before, it may be a good idea to get a more experienced gun owner or someone at the shooting range you will be using to help you out the first time.

Prepare

Before you start taking your gun to pieces to clean it, you need to select an area to work in.

- Well-lit.
- Well-ventilated.
- Lots of space to work.
- Large sturdy work surface free from clutter.

Tip: Don't clean your firearm on a surface that is used to prepare or serve food and drink. Cleaning materials and fouling removed during the cleaning process may contaminate the surface and any nearby food and drink.

Outdoors or in the garage are two of the best, safest places to clean your firearm. Inside your home is an option but it shouldn't be your first choice. If you must clean your gun inside, make sure you do so near an open window.

Tip: Remove any and all live ammunition from the cleaning area or room. Empty every gun magazine and store the ammunition securely in a different location until you have finished cleaning your gun. Removing all loose and boxed ammunition will help prevent any accidents from happening. After all, a gun cannot fire a round if there aren't any, nor can any cleaning tools or chemicals accidentally cause a round to explode if they aren't nearby.

Read the Manual

If you are the kind of person who usually dumps the owner manual to every appliance or gadget you own into the trash, do not do it with the owner's manual to your firearm. Make peace with the fact that you have to make an exception and keep this one. However, simply keeping the manual isn't going to do you much good, you have to actually read it as well, and not only the most interesting bits either. As a responsible gun owner, you should read the entire manual before you even pick up your new gun and fire it.

Gun Cleaning Tools and Supplies

Now that you have taken all the necessary safety precautions, it's time to roll your sleeves up and start with the maintenance. Bear in mind that different techniques will apply to different guns but there are some basic essential tools to the process of cleaning and caring for your firearm.

Cleaning Rod

The cleaning rod should be made from a softer material than the barrel of the firearm. The majority of barrels are made from steel and many cleaning rods are made of carbon fiber or aluminum. If the cleaning rod is made of a material that is as hard as, or harder than, the gun barrel, it could cause damage. Carbon fiber is one of the most popular materials as it is less likely to scratch the barrel. Bear in mind that even a carbon fiber cleaning rod risks damaging the firearm if used incorrectly. Even a small amount of damage to the crown can affect the firearm's accuracy.

Cleaning Jags

Jags are attachments that go on the end of a cleaning rod. Their purpose is to hold the cleaning cloth or patch in place as you push the cleaning rod into the bore. The way a jag works is to pierce the middle of the cleaning patch and push it through the barrel using the cleaning rod.

Cleaning Patches

Cleaning patches are small pieces of cloth used to clean the barrel of a gun. Always use a clean patch through the bore and change the patch every time the cleaning rod passes through the barrel. Cleaning patches aren't designed for multiple uses. Reusing one can actually transfer dirt back into the barrel instead of cleaning it.

Cleaning Brush

Cleaning brushes are pretty self-explanatory. One consideration for choosing a cleaning brush is that it must be made of materials that will not damage the inside of the gun barrel. Nylon brushes are suitable for general cleaning. For stubborn carbon build-up, you may need to use a bronze brush.

Cleaning Agents

Upon firing a gun, the internal parts of the gun are subject to extremely high-speed movement, extreme heat, and friction between the moving parts. The wear and tear that happens due to the regular use of a firearm make choosing and using the right cleaning chemicals vitally important. There are four basic firearm cleaning agents that will not only clean but also protect your gun.

- Solvent: Removes deposits of lead, carbon, and other kinds of fouling from the bore.
- Degreaser: Removes dirt and oil from the gun's moving parts to leave them clean for lubrication.
- Lubricant: Lubricates moving parts to protect against friction and rust.
- Protectant: Water repellant that prevents corrosion and rust.

If you are uncertain about brands and types of gun cleaning agents, consult a gunsmith or an experienced gun handler, such as a training coach, at your shooting range for advice and recommendations.

Utility Cleaning Brush

While you can technically use an old toothbrush, it won't be as effective as a gun utility cleaning brush that is designed to reach and clean all the nooks and crannies of your firearm.

Bore Snake

A bore snake is a quick and easy-to-use cleaning tool that will help prevent fouling and debris build up inside the bore and barrel of your gun. It resembles a lanyard that is coated with cleaner before use and pulled through the bore from the back and out the front. Never clean a firearm from front to back, always ensure that you are cleaning in the same direction the bullet travels.

Cleaning Kits

To make your job easier as a newcomer to gun ownership, there are a variety of cleaning kits available on the market and they're caliber specific. Each kit will contain the majority, if not all, of the cleaning tools and supplies necessary for basic firearm maintenance.

Additional Maintenance Must-Haves

- Cleaning cradle: Useful for cradling longer guns so that you can use both hands during the cleaning process.
- Safety glasses: Important for eye protection against debris, accidentally flying springs, or potential cleaning agent splashes.
- Solvent-resistant gloves: Protect your hands from harmful chemicals while cleaning your firearm.

Basic Gun Cleaning

As previously stated, always follow the manufacturer manual for cleaning and handling your firearm. The steps listed below are only a general guideline for the basic cleaning of a firearm and do not supersede the manual and manufacturer's instructions.

Note: Before you start disassembling a firearm for maintenance, remove the magazine and check for any chambered rounds. Ensure that the gun is completely unloaded before doing anything else.

Semi Automatic Pistols

- Clean the barrel and chamber by using a nylon or copper-phosphate bore brush. Brush in the direction from chamber to muzzle. Dry brushing will dislodge and get rid of some of the metal and carbon fouling.

- Dip a cleaning patch into the solvent and pierce it with the jag on the end of your cleaning rod. Using a chamber to muzzle direction, push the cleaning patch through the barrel until it comes out the other end. This will cover the internal surfaces of the chamber and bore with solvent.
- Don't pull the patch back through the barrel as this will bring dislodged dirt back into the gun.
- Allow your gun to rest for 10 to 15 minutes so that the solvent can break down the fouling.
- After the resting time is up, use a bore brush to clean the inside of the gun barrel.
- After scrubbing the barrel, push a clean and dry cleaning patch through the barrel with the cleaning rod. Repeat this step, using a new cleaning patch each time, until the patch comes out clean on the other side.
- Use a pull-through tool, like a bore snake, covered in a light lubricant, pulling it through from chamber to muzzle, to lubricate the bore. This cleans and helps protect the inner surfaces from corrosion. Do not use gun oil to lubricate the bore.
- Clean the outside of the gun barrel, barrel hood, and lung, and the feed ramp of the firearm.
- Clean the action and lubricate it. You can clean the action using a nylon utility brush, a dry cloth, and a liberal amount of action cleaning solvent.
- Allow all the disassembled parts of the gun to dry thoroughly.
- The final step for cleaning your firearm is to use a needle applicator for precise lubricant application to the outside of the barrel, slide assembly, and action as per the manufacturer's instructions. Avoid over lubrication.
- Consult the manual for exact instructions on cleaning the magazine of your particular firearm.

- Reassemble the gun and give it a functional check to make sure everything is working as it should. Pay attention to the function of the safety, trigger mechanism, locking, slide operation, and the retention and ejection of the magazine.
- Wipe the outside of the gun down with a gun or reel cloth. They are pre-treated with a silicone-based lubricant which will remove any remaining dirt or contaminants on the exterior.

Swing-Out Revolvers

- Cleaning a revolver follows a very similar procedure to that of cleaning a semi-automatic pistol. Follow all the same pre-cleaning safety precautions to avoid unnecessary accidents.
- Open the cylinder by swinging it out to the side. Clean the barrel by using a nylon or copper-phosphate bore brush. Brush in the direction from cylinder to muzzle. Dry brushing will dislodge and get rid of some of the metal and carbon fouling. Be sure to cover the cylinder with an old sock or a piece of cloth to avoid any potential damage while cleaning the barrel.
- Dip a cleaning patch into the solvent and pierce it with the jag on the end of your cleaning rod. Using a chamber to muzzle direction, push the cleaning patch through the barrel until it comes out the other end. This will cover the internal surfaces of the barrel with solvent.
- Don't pull the patch back through the barrel as this will bring dislodged dirt back into the gun.
- Allow your gun to rest for 10 to 15 minutes so that the solvent can break down the fouling.
- After the resting time is up, use a bore brush to clean the inside of the gun barrel.
- After scrubbing the barrel, push a clean and dry cleaning patch through the barrel with the cleaning rod. Repeat this step, using

a new cleaning patch every time, until the cleaning patch comes out clean on the other side.

- Use a pull-through tool, like a bore snake, covered in a light lubricant, pulling it through from cylinder to muzzle, to lubricate the bore. This cleans and helps to protect the inner surfaces from corrosion. Do not use gun oil to lubricate the barrel.
- Using a gentle brush again, clean each chamber of the cylinder as well as both ends. Again, use cleaning patches dipped in solvent after brushing and then dry cleaning patches to clear any residual dirt.
- Allow the gun to dry thoroughly.
- The final step for cleaning your revolver is to use a needle applicator for precise lubricant application as per the manufacturer's instructions. Avoid over lubrication.
- Wipe the outside of the gun down with a gun or reel cloth. They are pre-treated with a silicone-based lubricant which will remove any remaining dirt or contaminants on the exterior.

Tips for Firearm Maintenance

- Consider having your firearm serviced professionally one per year. A professional gunsmith will be able to pick up on subtle faults or wear and tear that you may overlook.
- Don't fit a heater of a light bulb in your gun safe. The stock of a long gun, such as a shotgun, could over-dry and crack.
- Don't pack your gun into your gun safe while it is in a gun slip, holster, or any other covering that will prevent free airflow to your firearm.
- If possible, avoid using multi-use ropes and rods for cleaning as they may easily become contaminated with corrosive acids and dirt.

- Always store your firearm in a clean, cool but not cold, and dry location as moisture is one of your gun's biggest enemies.

When to Clean Your Gun

The topic of when and how frequently guns should be cleaned is a controversial one. Much of it is dictated by personal preference. However, there are a few scenarios that fall into the category of should clean and a category of must clean.

Strictly speaking, you don't have to but should consider cleaning your gun in the following situations.

After Purchase—Brand New Gun

When you bring your brand new firearm home, it may look all clean and shiny but you should treat it as if it were filthy and in need of a good clean. Not only will you ensure that it is well and truly clean, but you are also familiarizing yourself with the firearm and its operational functions.

Purchasing a brand new gun comes with the assumption that everything is new and in perfect working order. It can be very tempting to just pull it out of the box and give it a go at the range. Cleaning is recommended but not essential and should you choose to not clean it before the first use, at least give the gun a thorough going over for potentially hazardous faults.

Firing Any Rounds

Many marksmen and hunters follow this practice as it is the best way to stick to a good cleaning and maintenance routine and ensure that you keep your firearm in good condition. After every time the weapon is fired, it should be cleaned. That's not to say that you have to take it to pieces and clean it on the spot. However, you should get into the habit of cleaning your gun when you get home from a hunting trip or a trip to the range.

The majority of ammunition available commercially does not use corrosive primers. This means that firing off a few rounds without cleaning afterward won't clog the chamber and barrel with fouling. In this instance, you can get away with not cleaning your firearm after every single time it is used and not run the risk of shortening its lifespan. However, allowing yourself to slack off is a slippery slope that could descend into poor gun maintenance practices down the line.

Unused for Several Months

One of the most common instances of firearms lying unused for several months at a time is that of self-defense weapons. Any guns kept for self-defense should be taken to and used at the range on a regular basis. Unfortunately, that is often not the case, they end up lying in a drawer or locked in a safe for the sole purpose of "just in case." When you rely on this gun for protection, you should be cleaning and oiling it monthly to make sure it's in tip-top working condition. The last thing you want is a failure or malfunction when you need it most.

The above-listed scenarios are when you should clean but technically don't have to. The following scenarios all strictly require gun cleaning and maintenance.

Corrosive Rounds

Not all ammunition is created equal. There are some, especially cheaper bulk packs, which use primers made of materials that give off corrosive chemicals when ignited. The corrosive chemicals can cause very serious damage to the internal surfaces of your firearm, especially in terms of fouling and pitting the chamber and barrel. Pitting is when corrosion causes small holes to form in the metal.

Dirty Loads

Again, not all rounds are created equal. Even if the primers used aren't corrosive, you could still end up using rounds that leave behind more residue than others. Some of this residue may indeed also be corrosive and may cause the same kind of corrosion and pitting as rounds fired with corrosive primers. When shooting dirty rounds, even if you have only fired a single shot, the firearm should be cleaned and oiled as soon as possible to prevent damage.

Moisture

Moisture is a firearm's greatest enemy. Whether you are out hunting or have been to the range, if your firearm has come into contact with any form of moisture, be it mist, rain, fog, high humidity, or anything else, it must be cleaned and oiled as soon as possible. Moisture leads to rust that will compromise the structural integrity of your gun and affect its performance. Rust could also lead to serious failures and malfunctions which may end up being life-threatening.

Common Gun Cleaning Mistakes to Avoid

Whether you have a shotgun or a handgun, whether it is brand new or an older model, there are some common mistakes to avoid when cleaning your firearm.

Gasoline or Kerosene for Cleaning

You may, or may not, have heard the urban legend about World War II soldiers using gasoline to clean their guns. It may even sound like a cool trick but it's really not. Never, under any circumstances, use gasoline to clean any part of a firearm. Both gasoline and kerosene are highly flammable substances and should never be used on or near a gun. Not only could disastrous accidents happen, but they will also tarnish a firearm's metal finish or it could even damage or dissolve a shotgun stock or wooden parts of an older handgun.

Not Removing Cosmoline

Cosmoline is a light lubricant that is applied to a handgun or shotgun to preserve it, usually over long periods of storage. Before cleaning a gun that has been treated with cosmoline, always remove the cosmoline first before continuing the regular cleaning process.

Not Cleaning Every Part

Firearm maintenance may be time-consuming and not everybody finds it a therapeutic way to spend their time. It is important to read the manufacturer's instructions for cleaning your gun and not skip a single part as you disassemble the firearm. Attention must be paid while cleaning your gun, take things slowly, and don't rush. Ensure that you clean every single part of your firearm to prevent the chance of malfunction.

Not Treating the Firearm as Loaded

Always treat every, and any, firearm as if it is loaded. It is one of the rules for responsible firearm ownership and it applies to cleaning a gun. The same practices for responsible ownership should apply while cleaning. Don't point the muzzle at anything you don't want to shoot or destroy, even once you have emptied the chamber. Keep your finger away from the trigger while cleaning and when cleaning the trigger, ensure the muzzle is pointed in a safe direction.

Forcing Parts Back Together

Never force the parts of a disassembled gun back together in the reassembling process. If parts don't fit perfectly together, there will be a reason. Forcing parts back together could cause damage that could lead to a malfunction later down the line. If you find a part doesn't fit, disassemble the firearm again and begin putting it back together, checking the manufacturer's instructions carefully. If the parts still won't fit back together properly, contact the manufacturer.

Improper Lubrication

The moving parts of a gun rub together when it is fired. Proper lubrication is imperative to prevent excessive wear and tear and to stop the parts from seizing or overheating. Not using enough lubricant will cause greater friction between the parts. Using too much lubrication will affect the proper function of the firearm. You must know how much to use so that you don't under or overdo it.

Wrong Tools or Wrong Way

It is important, for the sake of your safety and the sake of your gun's longevity, that you use the proper tools for cleaning a firearm. Using the wrong tools could cause damage to the inside of your gun, causing it to malfunction or lose accuracy. Likewise, using the right tools the wrong way will cause similar damage.

Too Much Disassembling

Even if a gun can come apart further than the manual says it can, don't be tempted to do so. Disassembling a firearm may void the warranty or you could put it back together incorrectly. If a firearm needs more than just a regular cleaning, take it to a professional gunsmith who has the experience and knowledge to take it apart and put it back together again safely and properly.

Chapter 11:

Differences in Law for Open Carry

and Concealed Carry by State

Gun laws differ drastically from state to state in the USA and this could make it very difficult for anyone who legally owns a firearm to know where he or she is able to carry a firearm. This counts for both open carry and concealed carry, as well as what type of firearms are allowed in different states. The only way to avoid unnecessary problems is to educate yourself before traveling from your home state to ensure everything runs smoothly in whatever state you visit or travel through.

State	Open Carry	Concealed carry	Assault Weapons Ban
Alabama	Permitted in general, handguns must be in holsters. To open carry in a vehicle, you must have a concealed carry license. Firearms are prohibited in certain places: • School-sponsored or pro athletics events that are not related to guns. • Prisons • Mental health facilities • Government buildings	Allowed with a permit.	No.

Alaska	Permitted with the following exceptions where no firearms are permitted: • Correctional institutions. • Domestic violence shelters. • Courts.	All people above the age of 21 who may possess a firearm legally. No permit is required.	No.
Arizona	Allowed and no permit is needed.	No permit is required for anyone older than 21 who is allowed to possess a firearm legally.	No.
Arkansas	Is permitted without a license.	This is a "shall issue " state in that a concealed carry license must be issued by law enforcement if an applicant meets certain criteria such as being over the age of 21 and is either a US citizen or a permanent resident of the US.	No.

California	Prohibited in general and is a misdemeanor, with a few exceptions. Local ordinances and state laws in California are often in conflict regarding open carry.	This is a "may issue" state and the issue of a concealed carry license is up to the discretion of law enforcement.	Yes.
Colorado	Permitted and no license is required, with the exception of local ordinances that contradict this in certain cases.	It is allowed and a permit is required.	No, with exceptions where local ordinances have banned assault weapons, such as in Denver.
Connecticut	Long guns – no permit required. Handguns – permit required.	Allowed with a permit.	Partial.
Delaware	Allowed without the need for a	Allowed with a	No.

	permit.	permit.	

Florida	Prohibited in general, although allowed for the following activities: • Target shooting. • While hunting. • Camping. • While attending a gun show. • Fishing.	Allowed with a permit, but prohibited in the following places: • Polling stations. • Police stations. • Bars. • Airports. • Courthouses.	No.
Georgia	No permit required for long guns, but a permit is required for handguns	Handguns require a permit, while long guns do not require a permit.	No.

Hawaii	Please note that although open carry is allowed with a permit, the police very seldom issue a license. An exception may be made and a permit granted by the chief of police if an applicant can show clearly that he/she is engaged in the protection of their property and life.	If an applicant can show good reasons that there is a fear of injury to his/her property or person, the chief of police may make an exception.	No.
Idaho	Allowed without the need for a permit.	Allowed without needing a permit, but with restrictions.	No.
Illinois	Prohibited in general.	Authorized with a permit, but with several prohibitions such as in bars, government, buildings, public transportation, schools, and others.	No.

Indiana	Allowed, must have a permit.	Allowed, with the issue of a permit.	No.
Iowa	Legal, with a permit.	Legal and must have a permit.	No.
Kansas	Allowed without the need for a permit.	Permitless concealed carry but must be 21.	No.
Kentucky	Allowed, no permit needed.	Allowed without a permit to anyone 21 and above who qualifies to legally own a firearm.	No.
Louisiana	Allowed and no permit needed.	This is a "shall issue" state. Local law enforcement will issue a permit for concealed carry on condition that the application meets the following requirements: • 21 years or older. • A resident of the state of Louisiana.	No.

State	Open Carry	Concealed Carry	Permit Required
Maine	Allowed and no permit is needed.	Anyone at the age of 21 or older is allowed to conceal carry without a permit as long as the person is eligible to possess a firearm.	No.
Maryland	Allowed, must have a permit.	"May issue" state. Note that permits are very difficult to obtain in this state. Applicants must be able to demonstrate a substantial and good reason as to why he/she should carry a handgun.	Yes.
Massachusetts	Entitled to open carry with a permit.	A "may issue" state. Concealed carry permits must be approved by the local authorities.	Yes.
Michigan	Allowed, a permit is not needed.	A "shall issue" state. Authorities will issue a license on the condition that the applicant meets certain stipulations.	No.

Minnesota	Open carry is allowed with a permit.	A "shall issue" state. Applicants must meet certain criteria before a license will be issued.	No.
Mississippi	Allowed without the need for a permit. The state places a prohibition on anyone who displays the weapon in a threatening, angry, or rude manner when he/she is in the company of three or more people.	Allowed without a permit, but concealed carry is forbidden in places such as bars, airports, government buildings, places of worship, schools etcetera.	No.
Missouri	Allowed, no permit needed.	Authorized without a permit.	No.
Montana	Allowed, no permit is needed.	This is a "shall issue" state. If an applicant meets specific qualifications, the local law enforcement will issue a concealed-carry license.	No.

Nebraska	Allowed, no permit needed. Take note that local governments may place restrictions on this.	Nebraska is another "shall issue" state, and if an applicant fulfills certain qualifications, the local law enforcement will issue a concealed-carry license.	No.
Nevada	Allowed, no permit needed.	A 'shall issue" state. Local law enforcement must issue a permit if the applicant meets specific qualifications.	No.
New Hampshire	Open-carry without a permit is allowed.	No permit is needed to conceal-carry a firearm.	No.
New Jersey	Allowed but must have a permit.	Allowed with a permit. Note that this is a "may issue" state and permits are granted at the discretion of the local law enforcement and they rarely grant permits to members of the general population.	Yes.

New Mexico	It is allowed without a permit.	This is a "shall issue" state and a concealed-carry license will be granted if the applicant meets specific qualifications.	No.
New York	The open carry of all handguns is prohibited in general.	This is a "may issue" state. Please note that it is very hard, in general, to acquire a license in the urban areas. The issue of a license is at the discretion of local law enforcement.	Yes.
North Carolina	Allowed without a permit. Local ordinances can however place restrictions on this.	Law enforcement must issue a license if an applicant meets specific qualifications as this is a "shall issue" state.	No.
North Dakota	Allowed. Handguns need a permit. Long guns in general do not need permits.	Permissible without a permit.	No.

| Ohio | Yes, it is allowed, and no permit needed. | Allowed if the applicant meets certain criteria as this is a "shall issue" state.

Important: there are certain restrictions and prohibitions that apply in Ohio.

• Any property owner has the right to ban all handguns from his/her property if they wish to do so.
• Concealed-carry is strictly prohibited on school property, government buildings, and churches. | No. |

Oklahoma	Allowed, no permit needed.	Constitutional carry was implemented in Oklahoma on November 1, 2019, which allowed both concealed-carry and open-carry without a permit.	No.
Oregon	Allowed, no permit needed, but note that this is subject to certain city ordinances. For example, in Portland, it is strictly prohibited for a loaded firearm to be open-carried unless the person has a concealed- carry permit.	A "shall issue" state. If applicants meet certain qualifications the local law enforcement must issue a license for concealed carry.	No.
Pennsylvania	Permissible without an open-carry permit. The exception is Philadelphia, where it is required to have a permit.	A "shall issue" state and as long as the application meets specific criteria and qualifications, law enforcement must issue a license for concealed carry.	No.

Rhode Island	Only allowed with a permit that must be issued by the attorney general.	This state has a hybrid of "may issue" and "shall issue" laws and permits are issued at the discretion of law enforcement.	No.
South Carolina	Open-carry is prohibited in general for handguns but is permitted for carrying long guns.	A "shall issue" state. Law enforcement must issue a concealed-carry license when applicants meet certain criteria.	No.
South Dakota	Allowed without the need for a permit.	Allowed without a concealed-carry permit since 2019.	No.
Tennessee	Allowed, but a permit is needed.	Allowed if the applicant fulfills certain qualifications and law enforcement must then issue a concealed-carry license as this is a "shall issue" state.	No.

Texas	Allowed as follows: • A permit is required for handguns. • No permit is required for long guns.	As long as applicants meet certain requirements and qualifications, local law enforcement has to issue a concealed-carry license as this is a "shall issue" state.	No.
Utah	Allowed and no permit is needed for unloaded firearms, but a permit must be obtained for open-carrying loaded firearms.	This is a "shall issue" state and a concealed-carry license must be issued by law enforcement when an applicant meets certain criteria.	No.
Vermont	Permitted without any permit.	Allowed and no permit is needed.	No.
Virginia	Allowed, no permit needed. Please note that certain of the cities have restrictions, always make sure that city ordinances may apply.	A "shall issue" state. Law enforcement must issue a license for concealed-carry if an applicant meets the criteria and qualifications.	No, but there are restrictions. (See restrictions listed below this table)

Washington	Permissible without a permit.	Allowed, but must have a license to conceal-carry. This state is "shall issue" and applicants will receive this license from law enforcement as long as they satisfy certain qualifications.	No, but there are restrictions.
Washington D.C.	It is illegal to open-carry in Washington, District of Columbia.	Allowed with a license issued by the Metropolitan Police Department.	Yes.
West Virginia	Approved without the need for a permit.	This is a "constitutional carry" state. Permitted to conceal-carry without a permit for people 21 and over who are authorized to legally own a firearm.	No.

Wisconsin	Allowed, and no permit is needed.	Law enforcement has to issue a concealed-carry license as this is a "shall issue" state as long as the applicant meets the qualifications as specified.	No.
Wyoming	Allowed without the need for a permit.	Allowed and no permit is needed.	No.

Virginia prohibits any person:

- Who is not a citizen of the U.S., or who is not lawfully admitted for permanent residence, from knowingly and intentionally possessing or transporting any assault firearms; or
- Who is a firearms dealer from transferring any assault firearm to such a person; and

From importing, selling, possessing, or transferring "the Striker 12", commonly called a 'street sweeper,' or any semi-automatic folding-stock shotgun of like-kind with a spring tension drum magazine capable of holding twelve shotgun shells.

Chapter 12:

Reciprocity Between States for

Carrying a Firearm Across State Lines

Gun laws differ from state to state, as well as having varying limitations for concealed carry permits. This could cause huge problems for any gun owner who wants to travel across state lines while carrying a firearm.

It is, therefore, important to have the reciprocity laws on hand for each of the states. This is not just for peace of mind, but to prevent legal battles in any state that you wish to travel through or visit.

Alabama

Alabama honors all concealed carry permits that have been issued in accordance with section 12A-11-85 of the Alabama Code from all other states except one. Out-of-state permit holders will be subject to the gun laws of Alabama while within the state.

Permits honored	Alaska, Arizona, Arkansas, California, Colorado, Connecticut, Delaware, Georgia, Hawaii, Idaho, Illinois, Indiana, Iowa, Kansas, Kentucky, Louisiana, Maine, Maryland, Massachusetts, Michigan, Minnesota, Mississippi, Missouri, Montana, Nebraska, Nevada, New Hampshire, New Jersey, New Mexico, New York, North Carolina, North Dakota, Ohio, Oklahoma, Oregon, Pennsylvania, Rhode Island, South Carolina, South Dakota, Tennessee, Texas, Utah, Virginia, Washington, West Virginia, Wisconsin, and Wyoming.
Handgun permits only honored	Florida.
Permits from districts and territories honored	Puerto Rico.
Permits not honored	New York City.

Alaska

Alaska honors CCW permits as set out below with the provision that all out-of-state permit holders must be 21 years, or older.

Permits honored (permitless carry)	Alabama, Arizona, Arkansas, California, Colorado, Connecticut, Delaware, Florida, Georgia, Hawaii, Illinois, Indiana, Iowa, Kansas, Kentucky, Louisiana, Maine, Maryland, Massachusetts, Michigan, Minnesota, Mississippi, Missouri, Montana, Nebraska, Nevada, New Hampshire, New Jersey, New Mexico, New York, North Carolina, North Dakota, Ohio, Oklahoma, Oregon, Pennsylvania, Rhode Island, South Carolina, South Dakota, Tennessee, Texas, Utah, Virginia, Washington, West Virginia, Wisconsin, and Wyoming.
Permits from districts and territories honored (permitless carry)	District of Columbia, New York City, Guam, Puerto Rico, and the Virgin Islands.
Enhanced permit only honored	Idaho.

Arizona

All out-of-state permit holders must be at least 21 years old.

Permits honored	Alabama, Alaska, Arkansas, California, Colorado, Connecticut, Delaware, Florida, Georgia, Hawaii, Illinois, Indiana, Iowa, Kansas, Kentucky, Louisiana, Maine, Maryland, Massachusetts, Michigan, Minnesota, Mississippi, Missouri, Montana, Nebraska, Nevada, New Hampshire, New Jersey, New Mexico, New York, North Carolina, North Dakota, Ohio, Oklahoma, Oregon, Pennsylvania, Rhode Island, South Carolina, South Dakota, Tennessee, Texas, Utah, Vermont, Virgin Islands, Virginia, Washington, West Virginia, Wisconsin, and Wyoming.
Permits honored from districts and territories	District of Columbia, New York City, Guam, and Puerto Rico.
Only enhanced permits honored	Idaho.

Arkansas

Arkansas is a permitless carry state. Any person who may legally own a firearm may carry concealed in this state without a permit or license.

Permits honored, minimum age 18 years	Alabama, Alaska, Arizona, California, Colorado, Connecticut, Delaware, Florida, Georgia, Hawaii, Idaho, Illinois, Indiana, Iowa, Kansas, Kentucky, Louisiana, Maine, Maryland, Massachusetts, Michigan, Minnesota, Mississippi, Missouri, Montana, Nebraska, Nevada, New Hampshire, New Jersey, New Mexico, New York, North Carolina, North Dakota, Ohio, Oklahoma, Oregon, Pennsylvania, Rhode Island, South Carolina, South Dakota, Tennessee, Texas, Utah, Virginia, Washington, West Virginia, Wisconsin, and Wyoming.
Permits from districts and territories honored, minimum age 18 years	District of Columbia, New York City, Guam, Puerto Rico, and the Virgin Islands.

California

California does not honor concealed carry permits from any of the other states.

Colorado

The Colorado law for out-of-state CCW permit holders are as follows:

- Permit holders must be 21 or older.
- Will only honor permits from other states if the state has already agreed to honor Colorado permits.
- Do not honor any out-of-state permits of non-residents under Section CRS 18.12.215 even if there already exists a reciprocity agreement between Colorado and that state.

Permits honored	Alaska.
Resident permits honored with minimum age 21 years	Delaware, Indiana, Mississippi, Missouri, New Hampshire, North Dakota, Oklahoma, West Virginia, Texas, Utah, and South Dakota.
Permits honored with a minimum age of 21 years	Alabama, Montana, and Wyoming.
Resident permits honored only	Arizona, Arkansas, Georgia, Idaho, Iowa, Kansas, Kentucky, Michigan, Louisiana, Nebraska, Wisconsin, North Carolina, Ohio, Pennsylvania, Tennessee, Virginia, and New Mexico.
Handgun permits only for residents	Florida.

Connecticut

Does not honor permits from any of the other US states at all.

Delaware

Delaware honors permits and licenses from other states with the following conditions:

- The issuing states must honor Delaware licenses to carry concealed deadly weapons.
- States must have a similar degree of protection as is provided by the Delaware licensure.
- States must not show a pattern of issuing permits and licenses to convicted felons.
- For states that issue multiple levels of licenses and permits' only permits that meet the requirements set out above will be honored in the state of Delaware.

Permits honored	Alaska, Arizona, Arkansas, Colorado, Florida, Kansas, Kentucky, Maine, Michigan, Missouri, New Mexico, North Carolina, Ohio, Oklahoma, Tennessee, Texas, Utah, and West Virginia.
Enhanced permits only honored	Idaho and South Dakota.
Only the Class 1 permit honored	North Dakota.

Florida

Under section 790.015 of Florida concealed carry license, this state will only accept permits from other states if those states agree to honor Florida concealed carry licenses.

Residential CCW licenses will only be accepted on the condition that the issuing state has a reciprocity agreement with Florida.

No non-residential licenses are honored, even in cases where Florida has a reciprocity agreement with those states.

Permits honored	Alaska.
Resident permits only honored	Arizona, Arkansas, Colorado, Idaho, Kansas, Louisiana, Kentucky, Michigan, Nebraska, New Mexico, North Carolina, Ohio, Pennsylvania, South Carolina, and Virginia.
Resident permits only honored with permit holder being at least 21 years old	Delaware, Georgia, Indiana, Iowa, Maine, Mississippi, Missouri, Nevada, New Hampshire, North Dakota, Oklahoma, South Dakota, Tennessee, Texas, Utah, and West Virginia.
Permits honored with an age restriction of at least 21 years old	Alabama, Montana, and Wyoming.

Georgia

Currently, Georgia honors valid CCW licenses from both residents and non-residents from the states that that in turn recognize permits from Georgia.

Permits honored	Alabama, Alaska, Arizona, Arkansas, Colorado, Idaho, Indiana, Iowa, Kansas, Kentucky, Louisiana, Maine, Michigan, Mississippi, Missouri, Montana, New Hampshire, North Carolina, North Dakota, Ohio, Oklahoma, Pennsylvania, South Carolina, South Dakota, Tennessee, Texas, Utah, Virginia, West Virginia, Wisconsin, and Wyoming.
Handgun permits only honored	Florida.

Hawaii

Hawaii does not honor CCW licenses from any of the other US states at all.

Idaho

Idaho is a permitless carry state, allowing any person who can legally possess a firearm, to concealed carry or open carry a firearm without a permit on condition that the firearm owner is at least 18 years or older.

All out-of-state visitors or travelers must have their concealed weapons permit or license on their person when carrying a firearm while they are in the state of Idaho.

Permits honored, permitless carry with an age restriction of a minimum of 18 years old	Alabama, Alaska, Arizona, Arkansas, California, Colorado, Connecticut, Delaware, Florida, Georgia, Hawaii, Illinois, Indiana, Iowa, Kansas, Kentucky, Louisiana, Maine, Maryland, Massachusetts, Michigan, Minnesota, Mississippi, Missouri, Montana, Nebraska, Nevada, New Hampshire, New Jersey, New Mexico, New York, North Carolina, North Dakota, Ohio, Oklahoma, Oregon, Pennsylvania, Rhode Island, South Carolina, South Dakota, Tennessee, Texas, Utah, Virginia, Washington, West Virginia, Wisconsin, and Wyoming.
Permits from districts and territories honored as permitless carry with an age restriction of 18 years and older	District of Columbia, Guam, New York City, Puerto Rico, and the Virgin Islands.

Illinois

Please note that the reciprocity of Illinois is constantly changing. Up till recently, they did not honor any CCW permits from any of the states.

Alabama is currently the first state whose permits Illinois will honor.

They do, however, issue non-resident concealed carry permits to travelers and visitors from the following states: Arkansas, Idaho, Mississippi, Nevada, Texas, and Virginia.

Indiana

Indiana honors the concealed carry licenses of all the other states. Licenses issued by foreign countries and other states are recognized according to the terms of the issuing state or foreign country, but this is only valid while such permit holders are not residents of Indiana.

Permits honored	Alabama, Alaska, Arizona, Arkansas, California, Colorado, Connecticut, Delaware, Georgia, Hawaii, Idaho, Illinois, Iowa, Kansas, Kentucky, Louisiana, Maine, Maryland, Massachusetts, Michigan, Minnesota, Mississippi, Missouri, Montana, Nebraska, Nevada, New Hampshire, New Jersey, New Mexico, New York, North Carolina, North Dakota, Ohio, Oklahoma, Oregon, Pennsylvania, Rhode Island, South Carolina, South Dakota, Tennessee, Texas, Utah, Virginia, Washington, West Virginia, Wisconsin, and Wyoming.
Permits honored from territories and districts	District of Columbia, New York City, Guam, Puerto Rico, and the Virgin Islands.
Handgun permits only	Florida.

Iowa

Iowa recognizes the permits/licenses from all the other states. They honor permits with some states as set out below.

Permits honored	Alaska, Arizona, Arkansas, California, Colorado, Connecticut, Florida, Georgia, Hawaii, Idaho, Illinois, Kansas, Kentucky, Louisiana, Maryland, Massachusetts, Michigan, Minnesota, Mississippi, Nebraska, Nevada, New Jersey, New Mexico, New York, North Carolina, Ohio, Oklahoma, Oregon, Pennsylvania, Rhode Island, South Carolina, Tennessee, Texas, Virginia, Washington, West Virginia, Wisconsin, and Wyoming.
Permits honored with an age restriction of 21 and older	Alabama, Delaware, Indiana, Maine, Missouri, Montana, New Hampshire, North Dakota, South Dakota, and Utah.
Permits from territories and districts honored	District of Columbia, New York City, Guam, Puerto Rico, and the Virgin Islands.

Kansas

As Kansas is a permitless concealed carry state, any person 21 years and older who may legally possess a firearm may carry it without a permit or a license. Therefore, all out-of-state permits are honored with the age restriction of 21 years or older.

Please note that all firearms must be carried in accordance with the specific gun laws of whatever state you visit or travel through. Always check the specific gun laws pertaining to the state you want to visit before going there.

Permits honored	Alabama, Alaska, Arizona, Arkansas, California, Colorado, Connecticut, Delaware, Florida, Georgia, Hawaii, Idaho, Illinois, Indiana, Iowa, Kentucky, Louisiana, Maine, Maryland, Massachusetts, Michigan, Minnesota, Mississippi, Missouri, Montana, Nebraska, Nevada, New Hampshire, New Jersey, New Mexico, New York, North Carolina, North Dakota, Ohio, Oklahoma, Oregon, Pennsylvania, Rhode Island, South Carolina, South Dakota, Tennessee, Texas, Utah, Vermont, Virginia, Washington, West Virginia, Wisconsin, and Wyoming.
Permits honored from districts and territories	District of Columbia, New York City, Guam, Puerto Rico, and the Virgin Islands.

Kentucky

Please note that Kentucky is a permitless carry state. However, all visitors and travelers must be at least 21 years of age for their out-of-state permits to be honored. All visitors and travelers must carry their firearms in accordance with the Kentucky rules and regulations.

Permits honored	Alabama, Alaska, Arizona, Arkansas, California, Colorado, Connecticut, Delaware, Florida, Georgia, Hawaii, Idaho, Illinois, Indiana, Iowa, Kansas, Louisiana, Maine, Maryland, Massachusetts, Michigan, Minnesota, Mississippi, Missouri, Montana, Nebraska, Nevada, New Hampshire, New Jersey, New Mexico, New York, North Carolina, North Dakota, Ohio, Oklahoma, Oregon, Pennsylvania, Rhode Island, South Carolina, South Dakota, Tennessee, Texas, Utah, Virginia, Washington, West Virginia, Wisconsin, and Wyoming.
Permits from territories and districts honored	District of Columbia, New York City, Guam, Puerto Rico, and the Virgin Islands.

Louisiana

Louisiana honors the permits issued by states that honor permits from Louisiana. The minimum age to legally conceal carry weapons in this state is 21 years. They honor permits from other states in two categories. They will honor permits as is, or they will honor permits with specific stipulations that permit holders must be 21 or older as set out below.

Permits honored	Alaska, Arizona, Arkansas, Colorado, Idaho, Iowa, Kansas, Kentucky, Michigan, Minnesota, Mississippi, Nebraska, Nevada, New Mexico, North Carolina, Ohio, Oklahoma, Pennsylvania, South Carolina, Tennessee, Texas, Virginia, Washington, Wisconsin, and Wyoming.
Permits with an age restriction of 21 and older honored	Alabama, Georgia, Indiana, Maine, Missouri, Montana, New Hampshire, North Dakota, South Dakota, Utah, and West Virginia.
Handgun only permit honored	Florida.
Enhanced permit only honored	Idaho.

Maine

This is a permitless carry state. If you carry a firearm from any of the states that Maine honors, you must be 18 years and older. Maine reciprocity falls into several different categories. For some states, permits are honored. Other states fall into the resident permits honored only, or resident permits honored with an age restriction and the last category is the permitless carry states which Maine will honor with an age restriction.

There are specific locations that are off-limits in Maine for any person who carries permitless in Maine. To carry your firearm as an out-of-state visitor you must either have a Maine permit or you must be a resident of a state that Maine honors.

- State parks.

- Employees' vehicles on work premises. Vehicles that have firearms inside them must be locked at all times and firearms must be placed where they are not visible at all.
- Acadia National Park.
- Regular archery hunting (deer only).

Permits honored	Alabama and Alaska.
Resident permits only honored	Delaware, Florida, Georgia, Idaho, Kentucky, Louisiana, Michigan, Mississippi, Missouri, New Hampshire, North Carolina, Ohio, Oklahoma, Utah, and Wyoming
Resident permits only, honored with age restriction of 21 and older	Arizona, Iowa, Kansas, Nebraska, North Dakota, and Virginia.
Permitless carry states honored, must be at least 21 years of age	Arkansas, California, Colorado, Connecticut, District of Columbia, Hawaii, Illinois, Indiana, Maryland, Massachusetts, Minnesota, Montana, Nevada, New Jersey, New Mexico, New York, New York City, Oregon, Pennsylvania, Rhode Island, South Carolina, Puerto Rico, Tennessee, Texas, Vermont, Washington, West Virginia, Wisconsin, and South Dakota.

Maryland

The state of Maryland does not honor any handgun permits from other states.

Massachusetts

Massachusetts does not honor the firearm licenses (LTC, License to Carry) of any other states.

Michigan

The state only honors resident permits from other states. The permit holder must be a resident of the state that issued the license. No non-resident permits are honored under any circumstances.

Michigan only honors resident permits from other states on the condition that the permit holder does not remain within the state of Michigan for longer than 180 days.

Resident permits only honored	Alabama, Alaska, Arizona, Arkansas, California, Colorado, Connecticut, Delaware, Florida, Georgia, Hawaii, Illinois, Indiana, Iowa, Kansas, Kentucky, Louisiana, Maine, Maryland, Massachusetts, Minnesota, Mississippi, Missouri, Montana, Nebraska, Nevada, New Hampshire, New Jersey, New Mexico, New York, North Carolina, North Dakota, Ohio, Oklahoma, Oregon, Pennsylvania, Rhode Island, South Carolina, South Dakota, Tennessee, Texas, Utah, Virginia, Washington, West Virginia, Wisconsin, and Wyoming.
Resident permits only from districts and territories honored	District of Columbia, New York City, and Puerto Rico.

Minnesota

The Department of Public Safety (DPS) of Minnesota is required by state law to yearly publish a list of the states that do not have similar handgun carry permit laws to that of the Minnesota permit-to-carry law. (624.714 Subd. 16). This list is published on the internet. The CCW permits from states on this list will not be honored in Minnesota.

Permits honored	Alaska, Illinois, Kansas, Kentucky, Louisiana, Michigan, New Jersey, New Mexico, Rhode Island, and South Carolina.
Permits honored with an age restriction of 21 years or older	Delaware and West Virginia.
Enhanced permits only honored	Idaho.
Class 1 permits honored with age 21 or older restriction	North Dakota.
Enhanced permits with an age restriction of 21 or older	South Dakota.

Mississippi

This is a permitless carry state, therefore all valid out-of-state firearms permits are recognized and honored of any person who legally owns and carries any concealed firearms, and includes the permits for concealed pistols, stun guns, and revolvers. The age restriction is a minimum of 18 and older.

Permits honored	Alabama, Alaska, Arizona, Arkansas, California, Colorado, Connecticut, Delaware, Florida, Georgia, Hawaii, Idaho, Illinois, Indiana, Iowa, Kansas, Kentucky, Louisiana, Maine, Maryland, Massachusetts, Michigan, Minnesota, Missouri, Montana, Nebraska, Nevada, New Hampshire, New Jersey, New Mexico, New York, North Carolina, North Dakota, Ohio, Oklahoma, Oregon, Pennsylvania, Rhode Island, South Carolina, South Dakota, Tennessee, Texas, Utah, Virginia, Washington, West Virginia, Wisconsin, and Wyoming.
Permits honored from districts and territories	District of Columbia, New York City, Guam, Puerto Rico, and the Virgin Islands.

Missouri

The permitless carry law of Missouri recognizes and honors all residential CCW permits from the other states and districts and territories. The conditions are that the person may legally own and carry a firearm and is the minimum of 18 years or older.

Residential permits honored	Alabama, Alaska, Arizona, Arkansas, California, Colorado, Connecticut, Delaware, Florida, Georgia, Hawaii, Idaho, Illinois, Indiana, Iowa, Kansas, Kentucky, Louisiana, Maine, Maryland, Massachusetts, Michigan, Minnesota, Mississippi, Montana, Nebraska, Nevada, New Hampshire, New Jersey, New Mexico, New York, North Carolina, North Dakota, Ohio, Oklahoma, Oregon, Pennsylvania, Rhode Island, South Carolina, South Dakota, Tennessee, Texas, Utah, Virginia, Washington, West Virginia, Wisconsin, and Wyoming.
Residential permits honored from districts and territories	District of Columbia, Guam, New York City, Puerto Rico, and the Virgin Islands.

Montana

The state of Montana honors permits from the states that do criminal background checks before that state issues a permit to applicants.

Qualifying permit holders who visit or travel through Montana must fulfill the following criteria:

- Must have photo identification.
- The permit holder must have the issued permit in his/her possession while in Montana.

Permits honored	Alabama, Alaska, Arizona, Arkansas, California, Colorado, Connecticut, Florida, Georgia, Idaho, Illinois, Indiana, Iowa, Kansas, Kentucky, Louisiana, Maryland, Massachusetts, Michigan, Minnesota, Mississippi, Missouri, Nebraska, Nevada, New Jersey, New Mexico, New York, North Carolina, North Dakota, Ohio, Oklahoma, Oregon, Pennsylvania, South Carolina, South Dakota, Tennessee, Texas, Utah, Virginia, Washington, West Virginia, Wisconsin, and Wyoming.
Permits from districts and territories honored	New York City.

Nebraska

Nebraska honors CHP permits from states that have gun law standards that are equal or greater than the gun laws of Nebraska as determined by the Attorney General of Nebraska.

The state of Nebraska honors out-of-state firearm licenses in nine different categories. It is very important to make sure in which category the issuing state falls to prevent any legal problems when visiting or traveling through Nebraska.

Permits honored	Alabama, Alaska, California, Colorado, Connecticut, Hawaii, Illinois, Kansas, Kentucky, Louisiana, Michigan, Minnesota, New Mexico, North Carolina, Ohio, Oregon, South Carolina, Virginia, and Wisconsin.
Permits from districts and territories honored	District of Columbia.
Permits honored with an age restriction of 21 years and older	Arizona, Arkansas, Wyoming, Missouri, Montana, Nevada, Oklahoma, Texas, Utah, and Maine.
Only handgun permits honored	Florida.
Only enhanced permits honored	Idaho and South Dakota.

Enhanced permits only with a minimum age restriction of 21 years old	Tennessee.
Standard concealed handgun licenses only (not provisional CL licenses)	West Virginia.
Only Class 1 permits honored	North Dakota.
Only non-professional licenses honored	Iowa.

Nevada

Nevada honors the permits from states that they have a signed reciprocity agreement with in accordance with SB 175 and AB 488.

Permits honored	Alaska, Arizona, Arkansas, Illinois, Kansas, Kentucky, Louisiana, Massachusetts, Michigan, Minnesota, Montana, Nebraska, New Mexico, North Carolina, North Dakota, Ohio, Oklahoma, Oregon, South Carolina, Tennessee, Texas, Utah, Virginia, West Virginia, Wisconsin, and Wyoming
Enhanced permits only honored	Idaho, Mississippi, and South Dakota.
Handgun permits only honored	Florida.

New Hampshire

New Hampshire honors out-of-state CCW permits based on three conditions.

- The permit holder must be a minimum age of 18 years.
- The owner of the firearm must be a resident of the state that issued his/her gun license.
- The permit holder's home state must be one of the states honored by New Hampshire.

Permits honored	Alabama, Alaska, Arizona, Arkansas, California, Colorado, Connecticut, Delaware, Florida, Georgia, Hawaii, Idaho, Illinois, Indiana, Iowa, Kansas, Kentucky, Louisiana, Maine, Maryland, Massachusetts, Michigan, Minnesota, Mississippi, Missouri, Montana, Nebraska, Nevada, New Jersey, New Mexico, New York, North Carolina, North Dakota, Ohio, Oklahoma, Oregon, Pennsylvania, Rhode Island, South Carolina, South Dakota, Tennessee, Texas, Utah, Vermont, Virginia, Washington, West Virginia, Wisconsin, and Wyoming.
Permits from territories and districts honored	District of Columbia, New York City, and Puerto Rico.

New Jersey

New Jersey does not honor the firearm permits of any of the other states in the US.

New Mexico

New Mexico only honors permits from the states with which it has signed a reciprocity agreement. New Mexico only has reciprocity agreements with states that have very similar gun laws to theirs.

Permits honored	Alaska, Arizona, Arkansas, Colorado, Delaware, Idaho, Kansas, Louisiana, Michigan, Mississippi, Missouri, Nebraska, Nevada, North Carolina, North Dakota, Ohio, Oklahoma, South Carolina, Tennessee, Texas, Virginia, West Virginia, and Wyoming.
Handgun permits only honored	Florida.

New York

The state of New York does not honor concealed carry weapons permits from any of the other states. The only exception is for pistol licenses issued in New York City, as this license is valid throughout the state of New York.

North Carolina

Concealed carry permits from all the states are recognized by North Carolina with only Florida having a type of firearm restriction.

CCW permits honored	Alabama, Alaska, Arizona, Arkansas, California, Colorado, Connecticut, Delaware, Georgia, Hawaii, Idaho, Illinois, Indiana, Iowa, Kansas, Kentucky, Louisiana, Maine, Maryland, Massachusetts, Michigan, Minnesota, Mississippi, Missouri, Montana, Nebraska, Nevada, New Hampshire, New Jersey, New Mexico, New York, North Dakota, Ohio, Oklahoma, Oregon, Pennsylvania, Rhode Island, South Carolina, South Dakota, Tennessee, Texas, Utah, Virginia, Washington, West Virginia, Wisconsin, and Wyoming.
Handgun permits only honored	Florida.
Permits honored from districts and territories	District of Columbia, New York City, Guam, Puerto Rico, and the Virgin Islands.

North Dakota

Valid concealed carry permits/licenses for both residents and non-residents of the states that have signed a reciprocity agreement to recognize the licenses from North Dakota are honored.

Permits honored	Alabama, Alaska, Arizona, Arkansas, Colorado, Delaware, Florida, Georgia, Idaho, Indiana, Iowa, Kansas, Kentucky, Louisiana, Maine, Michigan, Minnesota, Mississippi, Missouri, Montana, Nebraska, Nevada, New Hampshire, New Mexico, North Carolina, Ohio, Oklahoma, Pennsylvania, South Carolina, South Dakota, Texas, Utah, Virginia, Washington, West Virginia, Wisconsin, and Wyoming
Enhanced permits only	Tennessee.

Ohio

Valid concealed carry permits from all states, districts, and jurisdictions are automatically honored, whatever the age of the permit holder may be.

Permits honored	Alabama, Alaska, Arizona, Arkansas, California, Colorado, Connecticut, Delaware, Florida, Georgia, Hawaii, Idaho, Illinois, Indiana, Iowa, Kansas, Kentucky, Louisiana, Maine, Maryland, Massachusetts, Michigan, Minnesota, Mississippi, Missouri, Montana, Nebraska, Nevada, New Hampshire, New Jersey, New Mexico, New York, North Carolina, North Dakota, Oklahoma, Oregon, Pennsylvania, Rhode Island, South Carolina, South Dakota, Tennessee, Texas, Utah, Virginia, Washington, West Virginia, Wisconsin, and Wyoming.
Permits honored from districts and territories	District of Columbia, New York City, Guam, Puerto Rico, and the Virgin Islands.

Oklahoma

This is a permitless carry state and any person who may legally own a firearm and is 21 years or older is allowed to carry a firearm. Oklahoma law honors valid licenses issued by other states to carry concealed or unconcealed.

Permitless carry honored, must be at least 21 years old	Alabama, Alaska, Arizona, Arkansas, California, Colorado, Connecticut, Delaware, Florida, Georgia, Hawaii, Idaho, Illinois, Indiana, Iowa, Kansas, Kentucky, Louisiana, Maine, Maryland, Massachusetts, Michigan, Minnesota, Mississippi, Missouri, Montana, Nebraska, Nevada, New Hampshire, New Jersey, New Mexico, New York, North Carolina, North Dakota, Ohio, Oregon, Pennsylvania, Rhode Island, South Carolina, South Dakota, Tennessee, Vermont, Virginia, Washington, West Virginia, Wisconsin, and Wyoming.
Permitless carry honored, age restriction of minimum 21 years, for districts and territories	District of Columbia, New York City, Guam, Puerto Rico, and the Virgin Islands.
Permits honored with an age restriction of 21 years old	Texas and Utah.

Oregon

The state of Oregon does not recognize or honor concealed carry licenses from any of the other US states.

Pennsylvania

CCW licenses from other states that Pennsylvania has reciprocity agreements are honored in six different categories as set out below.

Permits honored	Alabama, Georgia, Indiana, Iowa, Louisiana, Montana, North Carolina, Ohio, Tennessee, Texas, Utah, Virginia, Wisconsin, and Wyoming.
Permits honored from districts and territories	Puerto Rico.
Permitless carry honored, age restriction 18 years or older	Arkansas, Idaho, Missouri, Mississippi, New Hampshire, South Dakota, and Vermont.
Residential permits only honored	Arizona, Florida, Mississippi, Utah, Virginia.
Class 1 permits only with a minimum age of 21 and older	North Dakota.
Handgun permits only honored	Florida.

Rhode Island

No gun permits and licenses from any of the states are honored by Rhode Island.

South Carolina

South Carolina honors residential permits from states that reciprocate with them. Permits and licenses of other states are honored in seven separate categories.

Permits honored	Idaho and South Dakota.
Permits honored with an age restriction of 21 years	Mississippi and North Dakota.
Resident permits only honored	Arkansas, Arizona, Kansas, Kentucky, Louisiana, Michigan, Minnesota, Nebraska, New Mexico, North Carolina, Ohio, Tennessee, and Virginia.
Resident permits with a minimum age of 21 years	Georgia, Missouri, Oklahoma, West Virginia, and Texas.
Enhanced resident permits only	Idaho and South Dakota.
Enhanced resident permits only with an age restriction of 21 years or older	Mississippi and North Dakota.

Handgun permits only and restricted to residents	Florida.

South Dakota

This is a permitless carry state. All CCW permits/licenses from other states, as well as districts and territories, are honored to carry permitless as set out below with an age restriction of 18 years or older.

Permits honored	Alabama, Alaska, Arizona, Arkansas, California, Colorado, Connecticut, Delaware, District of Columbia, Florida, Georgia, Hawaii, Idaho, Illinois, Indiana, Iowa, Kansas, Kentucky, Louisiana, Maine, Maryland, Massachusetts, Michigan, Minnesota, Mississippi, Missouri, Montana, Nebraska, Nevada, New Hampshire, New Jersey, New Mexico, New York, North Carolina, North Dakota, Ohio, Oklahoma, Oregon, Pennsylvania, Puerto Rico, Rhode Island, South Carolina, Tennessee, Texas, Utah, Virginia, Washington, West Virginia, Wisconsin, and Wyoming.
Territories and districts permits honored	District of Columbia, New York City, Guam, Puerto Rico, and the Virgin Islands.

Tennessee

All concealed carry permits from other states, with two exceptions as below, are honored by Tennessee with the condition that the out-of-state person who carries a handgun must at all times have their permit in their possession when carrying their firearms.

Permits honored	Alabama, Alaska, Arizona, Arkansas, California, Colorado, Connecticut, Delaware, Georgia, Hawaii, Idaho, Illinois, Indiana, Iowa, Kansas, Kentucky, Louisiana, Maine, Maryland, Massachusetts, Michigan, Minnesota, Mississippi, Missouri, Montana, Nebraska, Nevada, New Hampshire, New Jersey, New Mexico, New York, North Carolina, Ohio, Oklahoma, Oregon, Pennsylvania, Rhode Island, South Carolina, South Dakota, Texas, Utah, Virginia, Washington, West Virginia, Wisconsin, and Wyoming.
Permits from districts and territories honored	District of Columbia, New York City, Guam, Puerto Rico, and the Virgin Islands.
Permits honored for handguns only	Florida.
Class 1 permits only honored	North Dakota.

Texas

Permits will be honored from all the states listed below. There are restrictions on some of the states regarding age, or specific types of licenses.

Permits honored	Alaska, Arizona, Arkansas, California, Colorado, Connecticut, Georgia, Hawaii, Idaho, Illinois, Iowa, Kansas, Kentucky, Louisiana, Massachusetts, Michigan, Mississippi, Nebraska, Nevada, New Jersey, New York, North Carolina, Ohio (see restriction below), Oklahoma, Pennsylvania, South Carolina, Tennessee, Virginia, Washington, and Wyoming.
Permits honored with the date of issue or renewal after 3/23/3026	Ohio.
Permits honored from districts and territories	New York City.
Permits honored with an age restriction of 21 years or older	Alabama, Delaware, Indiana, Maryland, West Virginia, Montana, New Mexico, North Dakota, South Dakota, Utah, and Missouri.
Handgun permits only honored	Florida.
Only permits issued by the RI Attorney General	Rhode Island.

Utah

The state of Utah honors the permits from all the other states, counties, and districts providing the permit holder is 21 years or older. There is one exception where Utah only honors the handgun permit, and that is for Florida.

Permits honored	Alabama, Alaska, Arizona, Arkansas, California, Colorado, Connecticut, Delaware, District of Columbia, Georgia, Hawaii, Idaho, Illinois, Indiana, Iowa, Kansas, Kentucky, Louisiana, Maine, Maryland, Massachusetts, Michigan, Minnesota, Mississippi, Missouri, Montana, Nebraska, Nevada, New Hampshire, New Jersey, New Mexico, New York, North Carolina, North Dakota, Ohio, Oklahoma, Oregon, Pennsylvania, Rhode Island, South Carolina, South Dakota, Tennessee, Texas, Virginia, Washington, West Virginia, Wisconsin, Wyoming
Districts and territories permits honored	District of Columbia, New York City, Guam, Puerto Rico, and the Virgin Islands.
Handgun permit only honored	Florida.

Vermont

Vermont is a permitless carry state and honors out-of-state permits from all the other states, for both open carry and concealed carry, as well as from Puerto Rico and the District of Columbia, The only condition is that firearm permit holders must be at least 18 years or older.

Virginia

The state of Virginia honors all valid CCW permits of out-of-state permit holders with the following stipulations:

- The permit holder must be at least 21 years old.
- The permit holder has not had a concealed carry permit revoked in the past that had been issued by the state of Virginia.
- Permit holders must be in possession of a photo ID that has been issued by the US Department of State, or a government agency of any US state, or the US Department of Defense.
- Permit holders must carry their concealed carry permits on their person, as well as their photo ID, and must be presented when a request from law enforcement is made.

Permits honored	Alabama, Arizona, Arkansas, California, Colorado, Connecticut, Delaware, Georgia, Hawaii, Illinois, Indiana, Iowa, Kansas, Kentucky, Louisiana, Maine, Maryland, Massachusetts, Michigan, Minnesota, Mississippi, Missouri, Montana, Nebraska, Nevada, New Hampshire, New Jersey, New

	Mexico, New York, North Carolina, Ohio, Oklahoma, Oregon, Pennsylvania, Rhode Island, South Carolina, South Dakota, Tennessee, Texas, Utah, Virginia, Washington, West Virginia, Wisconsin, and Wyoming.
Permits honored from districts and territories	District of Columbia, New York City, Guam, Puerto Rico, and the Virgin Islands.
Handgun permits only	Florida.
Enhanced permits only	Idaho.
Class 1 permits only	North Dakota.

Washington

Washington has strict regulations regarding reciprocity and will only honor a concealed carry license from the states listed below under the following conditions:

- That the state of origin also honors Washington concealed carry licenses.
- The state of origin does mandatory checks based on fingerprints for the mental health history and criminal background of the applicants.
- That the state of original does not issue any CPL licenses to anyone younger than 21 years of age.

Permits honored	Kansas, Louisiana, Michigan, North Carolina, Ohio, and Oklahoma.
Enhanced permits only	Idaho and South Dakota.
Class 1 permits only	North Dakota.
Regular permits only, no provisional permits honored	Utah.

Washington D.C.

The District of Columbia does not honor concealed-carry licenses/permits from any other state, territory, or subdivision in the USA.

West Virginia

West Virginia is now a permitless carry state and in effect, any person who can legally own a firearm and is 21 or older, is now able to carry a concealed weapon without any permit.

Therefore, West Virginia honors CCW permits from all the states, as well as Puerto Rico, the District of Columbia, and New York City.

Wisconsin

Wisconsin honors the permits from those states that it has a reciprocity agreement with, as well as states that have background checks similar to the background checks done under Wisconsin law.

Permits holders from these states with CCW permits may concealed carry within Wisconsin providing that they are not residents of Wisconsin.

Permits honored	Alaska, Arizona, Arkansas, Colorado, Connecticut, Georgia, Hawaii, Illinois, Iowa, Kansas, Kentucky, Maryland, Michigan, Minnesota, Mississippi, Nebraska, Nevada, New York, North Carolina, Pennsylvania, Rhode Island, South Carolina, Tennessee, Texas, Washington, and Wyoming.
Permits honored from territories and districts	District of Columbia, Puerto Rico, and the Virgin Islands.
Permits honored	Alabama, California, Delaware, Indiana,

with an age restriction of at least 21 years old	Montana, New Mexico, Utah, and West Virginia.

Enhanced permits only	Idaho.
Class A permits only	Massachusetts.
Only regular permits (not provisional permits) issued or renewed on or after 8/28/2913 with a minimum age of 21 years old	Missouri.
Only permits renew or issued on or after 3/23/2015	Ohio.
Only non-resident permits that were issued/renewed after 8/1/2013	Florida.
Only permits renewed on or after 3/9/2015	Louisiana.
Gold and enhanced permits only with a minimum age of 21 years	South Dakota.
Class 1 permits only with a minimum age of 21 years	North Dakota.

Only permits issued/renewed on or after 10/1/2018	Oklahoma.
Only non-resident permits honored	Virginia.

Wyoming

The concealed firearm permit statute of Wyoming provides that permits from other states will be honored and those out-of-state permit holders will be provided with Wyoming permits under the following conditions:

- That the states of issue of the CCW permit also recognizes permits from Wyoming.
- That the permit from the issuing state is valid statewide.

Permits honored	Alabama, Alaska, Arizona, Arkansas, Colorado, Georgia, Idaho, Indiana, Iowa, Kansas, Kentucky, Louisiana, Maine, Michigan, Mississippi, Missouri, Montana, Nebraska, Nevada, New Hampshire, New Mexico, North Carolina, North Dakota, Ohio, Oklahoma, Pennsylvania, South Carolina, South Dakota, Tennessee, Texas, Utah, Virginia, West Virginia, and Wisconsin.
Only handgun permits honored	Florida.

Conclusion

Gun ownership is a fascinating subject that could fill volumes of books. You have been provided with a good starting point for expanding your knowledge of guns, owning them, using them, and the laws involved. The legalities of owning, carrying, and using a gun may be quite complex but safely handling a gun only requires a few simple responsible gun ownership principles to be followed.

Now that you have read this book, you have been equipped with an arsenal of knowledge. You've discovered what the 2nd Amendment really is and why it was created. You also know how the interpretation has changed over time and how it now affects you as a gun owner and handler in modern America. Isn't it interesting how laws that were created centuries ago are still governing our great nation today?

We've also equipped you with basic knowledge about the stand your ground laws, how the duty to retreat law words and that stand your ground laws don't legally negate your duty to retreat whenever it is safely possible when you're facing an imminent threat to yourself, your home, or your loved ones. Bear in mind that the castle doctrine isn't a law and doesn't entitle you to shoot someone, even if it is in self-defense, without exhausting all other options of safely resolving the threat first.

Concealed carry and open carry have been covered in such a way as to help you make the best choice between the two depending on local laws and your personal preference. Topics of gun operations, cleaning, and safety principles have been explained. We've impressed upon you the importance of proper gun maintenance and care and why responsibility is crucial in the ownership, carrying, and handling of firearms.

You've also been provided knowledge on firearms and their use for self-defense as well as some basic suggestions for responsibly handling self-defense shootings if you ever find yourself in that position. Now that you have a fundamental understanding of your responsibility as a gun owner, the laws that govern your actions when using a gun, and your rights, you are ready to start your journey as a gun owner. Get started putting this knowledge into practice today, starting with the principles of firearm safety and building your knowledge and experience from there!

Please remember that this book is in no way an exhaustive reference for the legalities and laws pertaining to owning and handling a gun. As a reader, you should not be consulting the information about federal and state laws or your personal rights contained within this book instead of consulting with a qualified legal professional. You should also not use this book as a training manual for handling and using a firearm. The information is meant to provide a basic guideline to supplement professional, certified firearm training. It is meant to provide you with a general overview of how a firearm works and the principles of using a gun. The laws and legal information in this book are correct, to the best of the author's knowledge, at the time of writing and publishing. That does not mean that the information is accurate for any length of time thereafter as laws and regulations are subject to change. Please always remain up to date with your local and state laws, federal laws, and the laws governing reciprocity between different states when carrying a firearm over state lines.

References

2nd Amendment 2017. (2017, March 6). *Robertson V. Baldwin (1897)*. 2nd Amendment 2017. https://2ndamendment2017.wordpress.com/2017/03/06/robertson-v-baldwin/

3 reasons why gun training is important for everyone. (n.d.) Pro Shots. https://proshotsrange.com/2020/07/06/3-reasons-gun-training-important-everyone/

7 gun cleaning essentials. (2018, March 26). Triggers & Bows. https://www.triggersandbows.com/7-gun-cleaning-essentials/

7 proven strategies to survive the legal aftermath of armed self-defense. (n.d.). Pathfinders Outdoor Adventures. https://www.pathfindersoa.com/uploads/2/6/0/5/26052768/7-proven-strategies-to-survive-the-legal-aftermath-of-armed-self-defense.pdf

A beginner's guide on how to clean a gun. (2019, October 18). Bill Jackson. https://www.billjacksons.com/a-beginners-guide-on-how-to-clean-a-gun/

Affirmative defense. (2020, January 10). Wikipedia. https://en.wikipedia.org/wiki/Affirmative_defense

Antebellum period. (2020,December 12). Encyclopedia.Com. https://www.encyclopedia.com/history/encyclopedias-almanacs-transcripts-and-maps/antebellum-period

Bigfoot Gun Belts. (2016, April 16). *A brief history of concealed carry laws.* Medium. https://medium.com/@BigfootGunBelts/a-brief-history-of-concealed-carry-laws-9b509778d254

Bilodeau, H. (n.d.) *The importance of firearms training.* Recoil. https://www.recoilweb.com/the-importance-of-firearms-training-129286.html

Boilard, R. (n.d.). *What you need to know when you own or carry a gun for personal protection.* Defensive Strategies, LLC. https://www.defensivestrategies.org/blog/carrying-a-gun-for-personal-protection

Carp, R. (2015, March 18). *First 48 hours: What really happens after a self-defense shooting.* USCCA. https://www.usconcealedcarry.com/blog/first-48-hours-self-defense-shooting/

CCW reciprocity maps. (n.d.) Guns To Carry. https://www.gunstocarry.com/ccw-reciprocity-map/

Cerebro SEO. (2017, December 7). *3 Reasons ongoing firearm training is so important.* Las Vegas Outdoor Adventures. https://vegasoutdooradventures.com/3-reasons-firearm-training-important/

Civilian marksmanship program. (2020, December 3). Wikipedia. https://en.wikipedia.org/wiki/Civilian_Marksmanship_Progra m

Concealed carry corner: Pros & cons of consistent open carry. (2018, December 14). The Firearm Blog. https://www.thefirearmblog.com/blog/2018/12/24/open-carry/

Concealed carry liability insurance for gun owners. (n.d.). Xinsurance. https://www.xinsurance.com/risk-class/concealed-weapons/

Defense of Others. (n.d.). Orange County Crime Lawyers Johnson Criminal Law Group. https://www.californiacriminaldefender.com/defense-of-others.html

Denning, J. (2015, April 9). *6 ways not to grip a pistol.* Guns.com. https://www.guns.com/news/2015/04/09/6-messed-up-pistol-grips

Duty to retreat. (2020, November 10). Wikipedia. https://en.wikipedia.org/wiki/Duty_to_retreat

Editor in Chief. (2019, May 20). *18 significant pros and cons of concealed carry.* Connect US. https://connectusfund.org/8-significant-pros-and-cons-of-concealed-carry

Findley, B. (2015, May 15). *Four pistol reload methods and nine magazine tips.* Ammoland. https://www.ammoland.com/2016/05/4-pistol-reload-methods-9-magazine-tips/#axzz6i47ErXMB

Findley, B. (2016, April 4). *How to rack a pistol slide: It's mostly technique.* Ammoland. https://www.ammoland.com/2016/04/how-to-rack-a-pistol-slide/#axzz6iIBpTW1i

Firearm maintenance. (2020, December 9). Wikipedia. https://en.wikipedia.org/wiki/Firearm_maintenance

Gaille, L. (2017, November 11). *10 advantages and disadvantages of gun control.* Vittana Personal Finance Blog. https://vittana.org/10-advantages-and-disadvantages-of-gun-control

Gharabaghli, S. (2020, February 18). *Why is it important to get firearms training?* Shooting Classes. https://www.shootingclasses.com/blog/posts/why-is-it-important-to-get-firearms-training/

Gontcharova, N. (2019, August 12). *Here's what you need to know bout the gun laws in all 50 states.* Refinery 29. https://www.refinery29.com/en-us/2019/08/239952/us-gun-laws-by-state

Gun laws by state the complete guide. (2018). Guns To Carry. https://www.gunstocarry.com/gun-laws-state/

Gun maintenance. (n.d.). Shooting UK. https://www.shootinguk.co.uk/guns/gun-maintenance

History of concealed carry in the U.S. (2020, December 17). Wikipedia. https://en.wikipedia.org/wiki/History_of_concealed_carry_in_the_U.S.

Isosceles stance. (2020, December 6). Wikipedia. https://en.wikipedia.org/wiki/Isosceles_Stance

Jackson, K. (n.d.). *Unload and reload revolvers.* The Cornered Cat. https://www.corneredcat.com/article/running-the-gun/unload-and-reload-revolvers/

Jones Webb, A. (2020, May 26). *The weaver stance - What it is and how it works.* The Lodge at AmmoToGo.com. https://www.ammunitiontogo.com/lodge/weaver-stance/

Jones, M. (2016, December 15). *10 common shotgun maintenance mistakes.* Buckeye Firearms Association. https://www.buckeyefirearms.org/10-common-shotgun-maintenance-mistakes

Justin. (2017, October 14). *RG101: Revolver grasp, or how to hold a revolver.* Revolver Guy. https://revolverguy.com/revolver-grasp-techniques/

Kenik, D. (2010, September 24). *The tactical draw.* Handguns Magazine. https://www.handgunsmag.com/editorial/tactics_training_hg_1207_06/138503

Kimberlin, J. (2008, March 5). *Open vs. concealed carry: What's the difference?* The Virginian Pilot. https://www.pilotonline.com/government/virginia/article_bf1 9b806-27f5-5c21-934e-ea7d0a803d00.html

LII Staff. (2018, May 17). *14th Amendment.* LII / Legal Information Institute. https://www.law.cornell.edu/constitution/amendmentxiv

Main advantages of laws that allow open carry. (2020, October 9). LTC
    Austin. https://ltcaustin.com/why-are-open-carry-laws-
    beneficial

Marksman. (2020, December 22). Wikipedia.
    https://en.wikipedia.org/wiki/Marksman

Mastering grip: 5 ways you're holding your gun wrong. (2017, May 18). U.S. &
    Texas LawShield. https://www.uslawshield.com/mastering-
    grip-5-ways-youre-holding-your-gun-wrong/

Mathers, J. (2019, June 19). *Concealed vs. open carry: Pros and cons.*
    American Gun Association; American Gun Association.
    https://blog.gunassociation.org/advantages-disadvantages-
    concealed-open-carry/

McLaughlin, G. (n.d). The fundamentals of handgun shooting. Black
    Ops School of Combat.
    https://www.drjkoch.org/Intro/Fall%202019/New%20files/F
    undamentals%20Of%20Handgun%20Shooting.pdf

Open carry vs concealed carry – Pros and cons. (2017, May 14). White Hat
    Holsters. https://www.whitehatholsters.com/about-
    us/blog/open-carry-vs-concealed-carry-pros-and-cons/

Pros and cons of the concealed carry revolver. (2019, September 27). JM4
    Tactical. https://jm4tactical.com/blog/pros-and-cons-of-the-
    concealed-carry-revolver/

Revolver vs. semi-auto pistols – Everything you need to know. (n.d.). GunPros.
    https://gunpros.com/revolver-vs-pistols-semi-auto/

Revolver. (2020, December 28). Wikipedia. https://en.wikipedia.org/wiki/Revolver#Loading_and_unloading

Rothman, L. (2017, February 15). *The surprising history behind America's stand your ground laws*. Time. https://time.com/4664242/caroline-light-stand-your-ground-qa/

Second Amendment to the United States Constitution. (2020, December 18). Wikipedia. https://en.wikipedia.org/wiki/Second_Amendment_to_the_United_States_Constitution#Debates_on_amending_the_Constitution

Semi-auto or revolver for home defense. Which is better? (n.d.). Ultimate Reloader. https://ultimatereloader.com/2019/01/16/semi-auto-or-revolver-for-home-defense-which-is-better/

Shaefer. (2020, September 28). *The basics of cleaning your gun*. The Art Of Manliness. https://www.artofmanliness.com/articles/how-to-correctly-clean-gun/

Sheriff Wilson, J. (2020, February 12). *Traffic stops: What CCW citizens need to know*. NRA Family. https://www.nrafamily.org/articles/2020/2/12/traffic-stops-what-ccw-citizens-need-to-know/

Shooting of Markeis McGlockton. (2020, December 11). Wikipedia. https://en.wikipedia.org/wiki/Shooting_of_Markeis_McGlockton

Shooting of Yoshihiro Hattori. (2020, September 30). Wikipedia. https://en.wikipedia.org/wiki/Shooting_of_Yoshihiro_Hattori

Should adults have the right to carry a concealed handgun? (2019, March 12). Procon.org. https://concealedguns.procon.org/

Sones, H. (2020, September 4). *Coaching for accuracy: Breathing techniques for staying on target.* Eley. https://eley.co.uk/coaching-for-accuracy-breathing-techniques-for-staying-on-target/

Stand-your-ground law. (2020, December 20). Wikipedia. https://en.wikipedia.org/wiki/Stand-your-ground_law#United_States

Survive—Legal aftermath self-defense incident. (2019, March 15). U.S. & Texas LawShield. https://www.uslawshield.com/self-defense-incident/

Team Armscor. (2019, February 4). Concealed carry vs open carry. Armscor. https://news.armscor.com/concealed-carry-vs-open-carry

The importance of gun care and maintenance. (n.d.) State Of Guns. https://stateofguns.com/importance-gun-care-maintenance-2764/

The top benefits of open carry laws. (2020, October 9). LTC Austin. https://ltcaustin.com/why-are-open-carry-laws-beneficial

Tyrell, F. (2015, October 9). *The dos and don'ts of gun cleaning.* Survivopedia. https://www.survivopedia.com/dos-and-donts-of-gun-cleaning/

Unloading semi-automatic pistols. (n.d.). National Handgun Safety Course.
https://www.handgunsafetycourse.com/handgun/studyGuide
/Unloading-Semi-Automatic-Pistols/601099_700077954/

USCCA: Self-defense knowledge, training & Legal protection. (2019). USCCA.
https://www.usconcealedcarry.com/

V. M. (2020, May 11). *Inspecting a new gun before buying.* Everyday Carry
Concealed. http://everydaycarryconcealed.com/inspecting-a-
new-gun-before-buying/

Volokh, E. (2014, December 26). *Self-defense is a constitutional right.* The
Washington Post.
https://www.washingtonpost.com/news/volokh-
conspiracy/wp/2014/12/26/self-defense-is-a-constitutional-
right/

Volokh, E. (2014, December 26). *Self-defense is a constitutional right.* The
Washington Post.
https://www.washingtonpost.com/news/volokh-
conspiracy/wp/2014/12/26/self-defense-is-a-constitutional-
right/

What states will honor my permit? (2019), Guns To Carry.
https://www.gunstocarry.com/ccw-reciprocity-map/

What to do in a lawful self-defense incident. (2018, July 9). CCW Safe.
https://ccwsafe.com/blog/what-next--what-to-do-after-a-self-
defense-shooting

Why is firearm cleaning important? (2019, October 11). Triggers & Bows. https://www.triggersandbows.com/why-is-firearm-cleaning-important/

Wikipedia Contributors. (2019, April 4). *Gun safety.* Wikipedia; Wikimedia Foundation. https://en.wikipedia.org/wiki/Gun_safety

Wikipedia Contributors. (2019, April 5). *Open carry in the United States.* Wikipedia; Wikimedia Foundation. https://en.wikipedia.org/wiki/Open_carry_in_the_United_Sta tes

Wikipedia Contributors. (2019, January 1). *Deadly force.* Wikipedia; Wikimedia Foundation. https://en.wikipedia.org/wiki/Deadly_force

Wikipedia Contributors. (2019, January 25). *American frontier.* Wikipedia; Wikimedia Foundation. https://en.wikipedia.org/wiki/American_frontier

Wikipedia Contributors. (2019, June 7). *Self-defense (United States).* Wikipedia; Wikimedia Foundation. https://en.wikipedia.org/wiki/Self-defense_(United_States)

Wikipedia Contributors. (2019, May 4). *Castle doctrine.* Wikipedia; Wikimedia Foundation. https://en.wikipedia.org/wiki/Castle_doctrine

Wikipedia Contributors. (2019, November 21). Presumption of guilt. Wikipedia; Wikimedia Foundation. https://en.wikipedia.org/wiki/Presumption_of_guilt

Wikipedia Contributors. (2019, November 28). *Concealed carry in the United States*. Wikipedia; Wikimedia Foundation. https://en.wikipedia.org/wiki/Concealed_carry_in_the_United_States

Wikipedia Contributors. (2019, September 5). *Handgun*. Wikipedia; Wikimedia Foundation. https://en.wikipedia.org/wiki/Handgun

Wikipedia Contributors. (2019a, March 17). *Shooting of Trayvon Martin*. Wikipedia; Wikimedia Foundation. https://en.wikipedia.org/wiki/Shooting_of_Trayvon_Martin

Wikipedia Contributors. (2019b, October 7). *Constitution of the United States*. Wikipedia; Wikimedia Foundation. https://en.wikipedia.org/wiki/Constitution_of_the_United_States

Wikipedia Contributors. (2020, January 4). *Gun laws in Vermont*. Wikipedia; Wikimedia Foundation. https://en.wikipedia.org/wiki/Gun_laws_in_Vermont

Wright, M. (n.d.). *Top gun care: How often should you clean your gun?* Trek Warrior. https://www.trekwarrior.com/how-often-should-you-clean-gun/

Made in the USA
Las Vegas, NV
07 January 2024

84018052R10144